Fabulous Forever!

A Woman's Guide to Feeling Joyful, Loving, and Free

Carol Chanel

Glo Fabulous Books · Santa Monica, CA
e-mail: glofabulousbooks@gmail.com

Cover art: Janet Davis
Editor: Carol Rosenberg
Cover and book design: Gary A. Rosenberg
Produced by www.thebookcouple.com

Contents

PART TWO
What Works to Feel Fabulous Now and Forever!

For Joyce, my friend, biggest supporter,
and true sister

Introduction

I want *all* women to feel fabulous. In fact, I've made it my mission as a woman and life coach to help women achieve this goal. When we feel fabulous, we are pure joy and pure love, and we are exceptionally beautiful. From that place of feeling fabulous, we create and live lives that are beyond our wildest imaginations. We have fun, and people want to share themselves with us!

The only thing that ever gets in the way of feeling fabulous all the time is a negative thought or two. It's really that simple. Fortunately, it's also simple to change those thoughts . . . forever!

I wrote this book so that you can read what applies to you and quickly discover how to change or shift any perspectives or old self-defeating thoughts that might be in your way and then learn what to do to feel fabulous forever.

The chapters build upon one another so that you can see

the progression of what it takes to feel fabulous. First, you choose to *want* to feel that way. Next, you remove any doubts, fears, or misconceptions about yourself as an individual and about yourself in relationships with other people. Then, you apply various concepts and new perspectives to yourself in and out of relationships in order to feel fabulous and maintain that feeling.

It is my sincerest desire to inspire you to know that you *can* feel fabulous and to give you the tools to be able to live from this powerful and joyful place. It doesn't have to take you long to shift into this new mindset. In fact, you can start right now because you've made the choice to feel fabulous just by choosing this book. That makes you a fabulous woman. Now you can build on that choice. Way to go!

Life is an amazing journey, and everything you've felt, learned, encountered, or been challenged by has made you a fascinating, complex, and beautiful woman. Now you get to truly live your life—every day—from that place. You can say with certainty:

I am a beautiful, fascinating, kind, bright, smart, wise, and loving woman. I am a Goddess, and I FEEL FABULOUS!

So let's get you started toward feeling this way every day for the rest of your life!

1

Ten Easy Steps to Feeling Fabulous!

Feeling fabulous is the most important thing you can do for yourself. While helping women learn how to feel this way over the years, I've discovered that there are ten steps you have to take each day to truly feel it deep in your core where it is long lasting. Before I explain the ten steps, I want to share with you what being fabulous really means and what gets in the way of it. This way, the ten steps will make more sense.

You Are Fabulous!

Yes, you really are. I'm not talking about the ego's idea of fabulous—the false or temporary sense of feeling good about yourself. I'm talking about the whole of you: your essence, your heart, your spirit, and your body. You are a spiritual being having a human experience. That means you come from Divine Source—loving, pure positive energy. That means you are Divine Source energy—loving, pure positive energy—in physical form.

What Is Being Fabulous?

It's an inner knowing of your worth, value, beauty, goodness, sensuality, passion, kindness, compassion, love, and joy. It's trusting yourself and Divine Source. It's surrendering. It's honoring all the qualities and values you brought into this lifetime. When you embrace your fabulousness, your life is filled with love and joy on a daily basis.

When you realize that you are fabulous, you become an irresistible magnet. Men love a woman who truly lives in her fabulousness. When you know it and exude it, your partner (or maybe a new guy you've wanted to meet) will want to be around you a lot. They don't care what size you are, how old you are, or what you wear. Healthy women also want to be around other women who feel fabulous. It's more fun!

What Fabulous Isn't

Fabulous women aren't mean, vindictive, petty, catty, jealous, cruel, hostile, or arrogant. They don't gossip about other women, criticize what other women wear, or talk down to people. They don't send scathing e-mails or shoot arrows at others or gang up against someone.

What Gets in the Way of Feeling Fabulous

The gremlin—your self-critical voice (your ego)—gets in the

way of feeling fabulous. In his groundbreaking book *Taming Your Gremlin,* Richard Carson shares how to quiet this voice. While Carson goes very in depth into how to do this, basically you just have to *notice* what the gremlin is saying, *realize* it's a lie, and then *choose* another perspective.

The key to realizing you're fabulous is to quiet the gremlin that criticizes you. When you listen to *any* self-criticism, you can't feel fabulous. So if you criticize your legs or your level of education or your upbringing or the school you didn't go to or the fears you have or your energy level—you are cutting yourself off from your fabulousness.

Why would you do that? Is it habit? Is it because it just feels familiar since so many women criticize themselves? Is it because you think the criticisms are true?

Well, they are all lies. Any criticism about yourself is a lie.

There may be things you want to change about yourself. If you can get started on those changes now, great! Lose or gain weight, further your education, take singing or dance lessons, tone your muscles—whatever you want to do, you *can* go do it.

The most important thing to do is stop criticizing yourself and get moving. The cost of self-criticism is exorbitant. The cost is self-love. I know. I criticized myself for years. And then when I stopped, I had to learn to stop criticizing myself for having criticized myself in the past. Oh, the ego is ruthless and tricky! Thank goodness my heart and soul won out over my ego, and now I am in a position to share what I've learned with you.

Whatever you do, don't expect a man (or anyone else for that matter) to help you get over your criticisms. They can't, they don't know how, and it's not their job. It's yours.

Remember: stop criticizing yourself. It's keeping you from love.

All of the love and joy you came into this world with as a baby is present in your heart and soul; somewhere along the line, you got disconnected from it. It's not hard work to get back in touch with it, but you have to be willing to do a few important things. In order to feel fabulous, you need to work on the three areas of your life—physical, mental, and spiritual. You can do that by taking the following ten steps for feeling fabulous every day.

FEELING GREAT ABOUT YOURSELF AND LIFE: TEN EASY STEPS

For lasting results—to feel fabulous forever—do each of these steps *every day.* Don't play small, complain, or listen to your excuses. Just do these ten steps. They're simple and easy. Honestly, you'll be thrilled with the results.

1 **Before you get out of bed, start each day with five minutes of appreciation.** Think of three things that put a smile on your face. They might be your warm bed, your pet, a good friend, a new pair of shoes, something you're looking forward to experiencing that day, and so on. What you're doing is starting your day in the energy of appreciation, which draws more things to you to be appreciative of during the day. Appreciation is a high, pure vibration that feels joyful and/or peaceful. What a great feeling for starting your day!

2 **Read three to five pages of an inspirational book.** Make yourself a cup of coffee or tea, sit down, and read

before you get busy with your day. It will add onto the appreciation energy and start your day with a more positive outlook, which creates more positive experiences during your day. I love books by Wayne Dyer, Esther and Jerry Hicks, don Miguel Ruiz, Eckhart Tolle, Deepak Chopra, James Redfield, and Colin Tipping. I could go on and on. I recommend starting with *The Power of Intention* by Wayne Dyer, then *The Vortex* by Esther and Jerry Hicks. I've included a list in the Recommended Reading section on page 159.

3 **Exercise from fifteen to forty-five minutes.** Every day do something physical, even if it's just stretching in front of the television while you watch your favorite show. Move your body. Put on some music and dance for ten minutes. You'll feel good physically and mentally too. Build up to thirty minutes or more a day. Your body needs to move every day, and by taking care of it, you will feel and look better.

4 **Eat *small* portions of healthy foods and chew slowly.** It's most important to have small portions. How do you determine what's small? Here's a suggestion that worked for me: When you go to a restaurant for dinner, eat half of what they give you and take the rest home for lunch the next day. That will show you what small looks like. People always wonder how I stay slim. I eat what I want, including a cookie every day, but I don't eat a lot at any one time. Remember, food is fuel, and you need it during the day. Breakfast is crucial—it's the most important meal of the day. It's your fuel for the first part of the day. When you have a good breakfast, you're less likely to overeat at lunch or snack on high-sugar foods.

5 **Wear clothes you feel fabulous in.** Don't wear anything you don't feel fabulous in. Give those clothes away. Have you ever noticed that when you go on vacation, you tend to take only your favorite clothes? If you wouldn't take it on vacation with you, don't wear it at home. That might seem shallow, but how a woman feels about what she's wearing affects her energy and attitude. If she feels good about how she looks, she's more relaxed, confident, and easy going. We all feel good about ourselves when we wear something that looks fabulous on us. If you're not sure what looks good on you, I recommend hiring an image consultant or stylist. I was lucky enough to have one get a hold of me when I was thirty-two, and she showed me what worked and what didn't in terms of colors, styles, purse sizes, skirt lengths, necklines, belt sizes, you name it. The right clothes and accessories will help you look fabulous. If you want to do some research before you make an investment in an image consultant, read *The Triumph of Individual Style* by Carla Mathis.

6 **Set aside quiet time every day to be silent and still.** Ideally, you will use this time to meditate—which, by focusing on the rhythm of your breathing, allows you to stop focusing on your mind's constant thoughts and quickly get free of the resistance your mind creates. Why is that important? Our resistance is what blocks us from positive energy, positive experiences, and positive people having a positive impact on our lives. Listen to a relaxing CD. Give yourself permission to relax—ten to fifteen minutes of relaxation will make a huge difference in how you feel and think. You'll be more centered, more creative, calmer, and your thought process will be clearer, which will help you when you need to make decisions.

For those times when you're really stressed and just can't calm down, I want to share a powerful and highly effective breathing exercise I learned from the yogis I've studied with over the years. This really works. I use it myself and guide my clients and friends through it when they are highly stressed. The good news is you can do it anywhere—even in a meeting; no one will be the wiser.

Breathing Exercise

Just close your eyes and breathe in and out. Keep breathing in and out. Do that five times. Then exhale to a count of three. Then inhale to a count of three. Keep doing that for five minutes. Ultimately, you want to get your inhale and exhale capacity to a point where you can do the breathing to a count of ten. A good way to do that is to increase the length of your exhale and inhale on a weekly basis. Go from a count of three to a count of five, until you can do that for five minutes. Then, increase the length of your exhale and inhale to a count of seven, then go to ten. Keep increasing the duration of your exhale and inhale until you can do each one for ten seconds for a total of five minutes. Then once you can do that, you'll want to hold your breathe for a count of ten between the inhale and the exhale. So exhale to a count of ten, inhale to a count of ten, and then hold your breathe for a count of ten. Then repeat the process ten times. You will be a new person if you do this on a regular basis. I have always been a high-energy person and used to get stressed from taking on too much and putting too much pressure on myself. I guarantee this works.

7 **Pray.** Prayer is one of the most powerful choices we can make to help us know we aren't alone. When you pray, it helps you to remember that you are connected to Divine Source. It allows you to turn things over to Divine Source (or "God"; use whatever word feels best to you), especially the things that are out of your control, which is true about a lot of things in life. Mostly, prayer allows you to feel Divine Source's love, which is ever present. Without taking the time to connect through prayer, we often forget or don't feel that love. So pray every day to stay and feel connected to the Source of all love and intelligence.

8 **Make sure you give love to someone.** This *someone* can be your cat or dog, a friend, neighbor, husband, coworker, boyfriend, and so on. Consciously giving your love to someone will put you in the consciousness of love. Giving love to others is crucial for the health and joy of your heart and soul.

9 **Give love to yourself.** Take some time to imagine that you are filling up your heart and every cell of your body with loving energy for yourself. Think of a kitten, puppy, or baby: they are so easy to love. They are pure spirit, joy, and love. Well, so are you. Maybe you've forgotten that you are mostly pure positive energy. You are a "spiritual being having a human experience," as Wayne Dyer and other spiritual teachers remind us. You want to make and take the time every day to give yourself the love you need. Love nourishes you, energizes you, softens you, and fills you with joy. Remember, you are a child of Divine Source. That makes you lovable and worthy.

10 **Before you go to sleep at night, finish your day the same way you began it: by being appreciative.** Spend a few minutes before you drift off to sleep verbalizing what you were appreciative of that day. You'll sleep better because you'll be more relaxed and positive.

I guarantee that if you do *every* one of these things every day for thirty days, you will significantly shift the way you feel about yourself. You will start feeling fabulous. Keep it up for three months, and you will feel like a Goddess.

Visualize yourself taking all of the necessary steps to feel fabulous. Tomorrow morning you will begin taking the ten steps, and you will be on the road to feeling great about yourself forever!

Choose to be willing to feel fabulous and to be irresistible. Choose to take the ten steps for the sake of the absolute joy of feeling like a Goddess for the rest of your life!

PART ONE

What's in Your Way of Feeling Fabulous?

All of us have self-defeating thoughts that get in the way of our success, our efforts, our heart's longing, our courage, and our willingness to try something new. Some thoughts allow us to move forward while others keep us stuck. That's what self-defeating thoughts do: they defeat us and keep us stuck in an old pattern.

In my coaching practice, I like to call those self-defeating thoughts gremlins. As mentioned earlier, this is what Richard Carson calls our self-critical voice. This is a productive way to make those critical, negative, demeaning thoughts less powerful. You can even learn to laugh at them eventually. These gremlins are the same thing as the ego. So whether we say it's your gremlin talking or your ego, these thoughts are just not helping you; they are hindering you. You need to learn to quiet the gremlin and replace the old thoughts with helpful uplifting and positive thoughts.

How do you know it's the gremlin talking? It's when you say things to yourself like "I'm stupid," "I'm ugly," "I'm a failure," "I'm a victim," "I'm unlovable," "I'm unworthy," "I'm not talented," and so on. Basically anything that is negative is coming from that pesky gremlin.

The gremlin creates a lot of excuses. Excuses are perfect examples of thoughts that keep you stuck in the same repetitive situations and behaviors. I am going to help you get unstuck by teaching you how to create and listen to new powerful and uplifting thoughts so you can feel fabulous and thrive this lifetime.

In this part of the book, I've included several chapters that offer you valuable insights into ways you might be sabotaging your spirit and joy and how to overcome those challenges. You can focus on the chapters that resonate with you and learn how to heal and free yourself from the wrath of the gremlin, or ego.

Only you know if you take things personally, or if you're too nice and would like to have better boundaries and feel fine about saying no when it's important. Only you know if you're a perfectionist and work too many hours on a project and end up not having any fun. Those are just a few examples of things that can get in the way of feeling fabulous. As I mentioned, you only need to focus on the ones that apply to you. However, if you're not sure if something applies to you, read the chapter. Sometimes the gremlin doesn't want to readily admit a challenge, and it might try to trip you up. Go around the gremlin and learn to overcome the challenge!

2

Learn How to Not Take Things Personally

Do you take things personally but wish you didn't? Do you want to know how to not take things personally? For example, if someone is rude to you or someone has a negative attitude about something, do your feelings get hurt or do you feel somehow responsible for their behavior? You know your life would be easier and less painful if you didn't allow your feelings to get hurt.

When I mention to people that I help my clients learn how to not take things personally, I always hear the same response: "Oh, I need help with that too."

So how do you learn to not take things personally?

People used to tell me all the time to not take things personally. I really wanted to stop; I just didn't know how. For example, the first man I really loved left me ("rejected" me) for another woman. How could I not take *that* personally? It certainly felt personal and a lot like rejection. I wanted to learn how people did it, how they avoided taking things like that personally. Did they have some secret system? Did they have a code, some kind of DNA that I didn't have? I searched for an answer, and here's what I learned:

The reason we don't need to take something personally is because it's *not* personal.

It's *Really* Not About You

How can that be? Isn't the person who is standing there shouting at me and being rude to me saying something about ME? Isn't the boyfriend who just went four days without calling me saying something about ME? When my boss was really aloof and dismissive of me today, wasn't that about ME? Isn't it true that because my mother was unaffectionate and cold my whole life, she didn't love ME?

Do you see where I'm leading you with these fictitious questions? The operative word in all of these scenarios is "ME." And here's the key. Drum roll please . . .

When someone is doing or saying something to you, it is about THEM. It's not about YOU, or ME. It's about THEM.

So back to my story: the man who "rejected" me turned out to be a drug addict and an unhappy person with cowardly tendencies. He left me for a woman who was willing to take care of him financially because he couldn't take care of himself. When I ran into him years later, I realized that I'd been spared a life of misery. (Thank you, God.)

If you hear yourself saying, "I can't believe they did or said that to ME," you need to stop, take a deep breath, and realize you used the "ME" word about someone else's behavior. We make ourselves the important part of the interaction when the truth is the other person is making themselves the important part of the interaction, and that's why it's about them.

Why It's About Them

What I'd like you to understand is that people have wounds that stem from their life experiences. We all start out as innocent little beings full of love and joy. If someone is raised in a home with a violent and abusive father or an overwhelmed mother or a mean brother or a competitive sister or a hypercritical grandparent, then in almost all cases, those people left behind wounds and scars on the innocent little being(s) in their home. And as that little being grew up, those wounds caused or contributed to unhealthy behaviors such as acting rude, negative, angry, contrary, condescending, dismissive, or manipulative, to name just a few.

Since most of us weren't raised in completely healthy homes with highly conscious parents, we all have wounds. Even when someone's parents are healthy, it's more than likely that person will encounter teachers, other students, other parents, or other family members who aren't emotionally healthy and wind up inflicting wounds on the person. To sum up, growing up in an emotionally unhealthy environment with adults who have wounds and scars from their own parents and life causes wounds and scars in the children. It's a cycle that keeps repeating itself until people heal themselves.

If you could walk in someone else's shoes for a while, more than likely you'd be able to understand why they are aloof, protective, critical, mean, or act in other unpleasant ways. It's not an excuse; it's an explanation of why their behavior isn't personal. And it's to help you understand them, so you can stop taking things personally.

Healthy people who either don't have wounds (almost impossible) or, more than likely, have worked to heal their wounds don't behave in ways that might cause you to react because your own wounds are unhealed. Healthy people are kind, polite, reasonable, and understanding. They communicate clearly, take responsibility for their actions or mistakes, and look to see how they could have done something differently or better when things don't go as planned. They have good boundaries, and they respect your boundaries. They acknowledge your opinions, and they don't try to make you wrong or blame you.

On the other hand, unhealthy people are quick to blame and criticize others. They can be rejecting, nasty, aloof, and rude. They don't take responsibility for their actions, they don't honor your boundaries, they demean your ideas and input, and they might even yell or throw things. And all unhealthy people have one thing in common: they've been wounded, and their behavior is almost always a result of those wounds.

That's why what someone does or says isn't personal. It isn't about you; it's about their wounds and their reaction because of those wounds.

Some Real-Life Examples

Let's take a look at some of my clients' real-life examples of how they overcame taking things personally. Consider the example of a client who had an aloof and condescending boss. She said he was "the most abrupt man in the world." She believed it said something about her. But what it said was something about him: he was condescending, abrupt, contemptuous, and overworked. Through her coaching work with me, she ultimately accepted that his behaviour wasn't personal, and it didn't work for her to be intimidated by him. When you can say, "This doesn't work for me," you become empowered. But as long as you continue to take it personally, you will feel bad about yourself and won't have the courage to change your situation.

By the way, one day this particular client gave it right back to her boss. In other words, she stood up for herself, and their whole dynamic shifted. He wasn't a bad guy; he was just a bully . . . as long as he was permitted to get away with it. He didn't have a large enough support staff, so he was often irritated and cranky from being overworked. My client and her boss now have a good working relationship.

About twenty years ago, I had gotten a job I really coveted. I was so happy and loved my work. At some point, the company was restructured, and I started reporting to a new boss who had serious personal problems that I was unaware of at the time. He was extremely mean, and I started having real problems working with this man. I was crushed. One of the directors told me not to take his behavior personally, but I couldn't understand how it was *not* personal. It wasn't until years later, long after I had left that job, that I learned that the guy had done some unbelievably underhanded things to the president of the company when he didn't get his way. Guess what? His behavior toward me *wasn't* personal. The man was imbalanced and manipulative.

One of my male clients was deeply in love with a woman who wasn't available. She would draw him in and then do something to push him away. (This behavior is commonly called sabotaging the relationship.) At first, he took this very personally. And here's why: He had done some things in the relationship out of fear that he felt guilty about. So he was sure her behavior was personal. In our coaching sessions, he looked at why he had done certain things, and he grew to be deeply sorry for what he'd done. We worked on his forgiveness of himself and on having him stop judging himself for his previous behavior. He went to her to apologize.

At first she accepted the apology, and everything seemed okay until she pushed him away again. This is when he started to understand that she had major issues surrounding emotional intimacy. It *wasn't* personal. She'd had a pretty tough life, and the way she protected herself when she felt unsafe was to lash out and push people away. And she was highly effective! Who could blame her?

Maybe you've been with someone who is affectionate and seems to be interested in having a committed relationship, and then all of a sudden they pull away when the intimacy gets too real. That person may be suffering from shame caused by some abuse or a problem from their upbringing. We often will never know the real reason.

It's rarely personal when someone pulls away. They are

afraid of being exposed. They try to protect themselves from being hurt. The more I coach, the more I see how shame plays an enormous role in messing up people's lives, especially their relationships.

Do you see now that people's behavior and actions are about them? If you go up and hit someone and they hit you back, well that's a different story. You might decide to take their reaction (their hit) personally; however, in that case, you provoked it. I'm talking about the unprovoked action or behavior—the yelling, the pulling or pushing away, the aloof treatment, the manipulations, or the overreaction.

A Tool to Ensure You Don't Take Things Personally

Here's a big secret about how to not take things personally: Work on yourself to heal your wounds. As we heal, we begin to see that other people have wounds that cause them to act or react in all sorts of ways. Often we can't *see* the other person if our wounds are too tender. They inadvertently hit a raw spot, and we react from the pain.

Let me give you a personal example—the reason I was so sensitive to the "mean" boss I mentioned earlier was because of the lessons I'd learned from my father and stepmother during my upbringing. They both had extremely difficult and borderline abusive parents and didn't know how to parent. At times they were mean, aloof, and critical, as well as emotionally and somewhat physically abusive. They passed their fears and wounds on to me. Once I healed my wounds, I realized that their treatment of me was a sad reflection of how they felt about themselves and how they were treated.

As we heal, there are fewer and fewer raw spots for others to hit and hurt. There are fewer opportunities and reasons for us to react.

So the two ways to not take things personally are:

1. Remember it's not about you—it's about them.

2. Heal your wounds. Then the things people say and do won't hurt you.

While you are healing and growing, please remember when you hear yourself say: "Why did she/he do or say that to ME?" to take the ME out of the sentence. Change it to "Why did they do or say that to THEMSELVES?" And realize you might not know the answer to that question.

My stepmother recently died. She and I had had an extremely difficult, painful relationship when I was growing up. And, fortunately, I had worked to heal the pain and hurt and had repaired our relationship. After she died, I found out something that was shocking and upsetting about her upbringing. Then her behavior and treatment of me made perfect sense. I remember I doubled over and cried. If only I had known. If only she could have told us, her life and all our lives would have been so different. And yet I'm thankful for the gift of our difficult relationship. I learned firsthand that it wasn't personal. None of the things she did or said were personal; they were reactions from that wounded place inside her.

You are not a victim of anyone's behavior or words. If you

feel like you are, find a coach, therapist, or healer and work through those issues that leave you feeling victimized. If you feel like a victim, then everything will feel personal. And sometimes, people are invested in being victims—it's a pattern of behavior that is familiar even if it isn't pleasant. Changing the victim thought process takes time, a major shift in perspective, and not judging yourself while you are working through it.

If you have been a victim of a crime or abuse, a licensed therapist is usually the best way to work through those painful feelings. And for the rest of us who have had experiences that led us to feel like victims on some level, just trust that you *can* change your perspective from:

"A Victim of Your Experiences to Victorious in Your Learning!"

Which will you choose? And please remember, IT IS A CHOICE. Will you choose *victim* or *victorious*? The next time you catch yourself taking something personally, try choosing to be victorious and see what happens. Ask yourself, "What can I learn here?" Tell yourself:

I choose to be victorious! I am loved! I'm a wonderful person! Here's to a victorious life and freedom from taking things personally!

— ⌒ 3 ⌒ —
Stop Criticizing Your Body!

Now that you understand that what others say and do to you isn't personal, and now that you've chosen to be victorious in your learning, I want to take you to the next step toward feeling fabulous: not criticizing your body. I've been wondering when this negative self-talk—this seemingly acceptable criticism of our bodies—started with women. We used to be goddesses just the way we were. What happened?

A few years ago, I was on a beautiful beach in Kauai looking at the magical turquoise water when I was confronted with my own thoughts of criticism. *Be quiet,* I told myself. *You're in Kauai—you've been swimming, snorkeling, hiking, and playing. So what if you don't look the way you did when you were twenty-six. You're fifty-seven and you look great.*

My ego had a few other little comments to make, and I just told it to be quiet and ran into the ocean to let my body enjoy the sensation of the warm water.

But I wonder, where did all this come from? I don't know one woman who likes her body or accepts it as perfect just the way it is, even when it is fit, healthy, and toned. Why do we need to criticize ourselves?

The yogis tell us: We are not our bodies. We are magnificent, precious, powerful souls having a physical experience in beautiful, feminine bodies!

Try having an exciting, loving relationship with a man when you have critical thoughts about your body. Men love our bodies; they don't notice our perceived imperfections—until we point them out. And they don't like it when we criticize ourselves. It makes them uncomfortable and want to withdraw.

We are all complicit in keeping this potentially harmful practice going. We will share our complaints with our girlfriends and receive consolation and understanding. We are passing it on to the younger generation. We consider it acceptable. It's not!

What if we were to just stop criticizing ourselves and started loving our bodies? Start focusing on the great things and forget about the things we think don't measure up to some standard of perfection.

Come on, we all know this supposed "perfection" standard gets created by men in the advertising industry using highly skilled photographers, lighting, airbrushing, tons of makeup, special angles, and the occasional woman who will look like the standard of perfection for a few years. But even she will have "flaws" the photographers will work around or airbrush out.

This is so endemic and out of control that recently the U.K. Advertising Standards Authority (ASA) banned two magazine advertisements from the U.S. cosmetics giant L'Oreal that featured Julia Roberts and Christy Turlington. It turns out that L'Oreal was unable to prove that the images of the two women hadn't been "overly airbrushed." The ads were banned for being "misleading" as well as for being an exaggeration. If you look at the banned ads, you'll see exactly why it's impossible for those women to look like that in real life. They look like dolls—impossibly perfect, not real. Back in 2007, L'Oreal ran a mascara ad that was also banned for falsely exaggerating the claims of one of their mascara products when it was discovered that the model—Penelope Cruz—was wearing false eyelashes.

If the U.K.'s ASA is fighting back, shouldn't the rest of us also fight back by not buying into these lies? We've all wasted enough of our time and our valuable energy focusing on the negative when we could rejoice in the positive.

We are Goddesses! You are a Goddess! Stand up and fight against this predominantly male advertising industry's attempt to manipulate us for the sole purpose of selling us products! We need to love ourselves and be appreciative that our bodies function. Remember, we are not our bodies. We are souls in these precious, beautiful bodies. We are beautiful! You are beautiful!

Choose to concentrate on all the great things about your body. When the ego comes in with criticism, tell it to be quiet or to get lost.

You can choose to feel like a goddess. You can choose to embrace the beauty of your feminine body. You can choose to love yourself. You can choose to strut your stuff. You can choose to feel and be sensual. You can choose!

— 4 —
What Does Your Self-Talk Sound Like?

In this chapter, let's broaden the concept of self-criticism to cover areas beyond how we feel about our physical bodies. Start paying attention to your self-talk. What do the conversations going on in your head sound like? Is your self-talk filled with love, appreciation, respect, humility, and integrity? Or does it contain negative thoughts, criticisms, judgments, anger, or disrespect? What do you criticize about yourself? How often do you do this? How does it impact your relationships?

There is one thing I know as a coach: people come to me because their lives aren't working and they aren't as happy as they want to be. And negative self-talk is a big reason why their lives aren't working and why they are unhappy.

Usually during the first coaching session I have with a client, I learn in what areas a client criticizes and judges herself or himself and to what extent. That mean gremlin says things that sound so certain and unchangeable! Quite often, most people who criticize themselves also criticize and judge others, which interferes with good relationships with anyone, but especially with oneself.

Since feeling fabulous is about how you feel about yourself, this is the place to start: learn what your critical mind (your gremlin) is saying, and change the dialogue.

One of my clients was in a job that required accuracy and perfection. Her personality was suited to those requirements. However, working in that job allowed her perfectionism, an already bad habit, to multiply. If things weren't perfect, she was debilitatingly critical—of herself, her friends, her family, and her boyfriend—until she didn't have a boyfriend anymore.

No one likes to be criticized, but I find this is especially true for men. I remember a male client telling me that the two things not to do to a man were: 1) not to judge or criticize him, and 2) not to make him wrong. Women don't like it either, of course, but men really hate it. They will either retaliate or shut down and ultimately leave. In my client's case, the man left. She was devastated.

I had her look at how hard, even sometimes nasty, she had been to him. And she began to understand why he left. Maybe a different man would have stayed around, but why would he want to? He knew her behavior wasn't personal. It also wasn't any fun for him. He wanted to be with a healthier, less critical woman.

With a lot of work on quieting her critical voice, she stopped criticizing herself, and that less judgmental attitude transferred to the other relationships in her life as well. She began to talk to herself lovingly and kindly, the way she wanted others to talk to her.

When we stop our negative self-talk and we realize that other people are talking to themselves that way too, we can become more compassionate, which allows us to have more fulfilling relationships.

Nine out of ten times, we learn to be critical while we are first forming our opinions about ourselves as children. We learn this behavior from the adults in our home, at school, or in our religious institutions. If we were criticized as children, we will be inordinately hard on ourselves. And again, if we are hard on ourselves, we will be hard on others.

For instance—what if your father insisted that you get straight A's and a B wasn't an acceptable option? And you worked to always get A's, but one quarter you got a B and your father demeaned and criticized you? As a result, you will more than likely be incredibly hard on yourself if you don't get the top rating, pay increase, or the best feedback.

You now expect yourself to be perfect. And you are unhappy with nothing less than perfection. It is impossible to achieve perfection, and it is a waste of time and energy. The desire to be perfect is all ego-based.

Some Good News

If we learn that we are engaging in a bad habit (for example, criticizing ourselves), we can unlearn it and replace it with a good habit. Thoughts become habits when we keep think-ing them. So start to replace those mean gremlin thoughts with nice loving thoughts. For example, "I'm stupid" can be

replaced with "It might be challenging for me to learn techni-
cal things, but I love the fact that I quickly grasp psycho-
logical and spiritual concepts." Another example is, "I'm
terrible at understanding finances." You could replace that
with "I can hire someone to help me understand finances. I
appreciate what I am good at understanding." We all have
areas that challenge us, and we all have areas that are easy
for us.

One of the big things I work on with clients is their relationship with everyone—spouses, friends, children, bosses,
and/or employees. And most of the time, the upset that
occurs in the relationship involves someone feeling judged or
criticized. And that makes everyone angry. And it makes for
disastrous relationships.

How Do We Change Negative Self-Talk?

The best way to change your negative self-talk is to cut yourself some slack. We all make mistakes. And the truth is your
father or mother or grandmother or grandfather or teacher
isn't here now telling you how stupid you are for making that
mistake. You've taken over their job. And that self-talk can get
really vicious. So stop! Follow these steps:

1. **Notice what you tell yourself.** Catch yourself when you
say, "You idiot, I can't believe you just dropped that glass!"

2. **Change what you say to yourself.** What would you have
liked your parents to say to you when you accidently broke
something? "Are you okay?" "Don't worry; we can always
replace that vase." "It's just a material item." "You are more

important." "Next time you'll know to use two hands." Say those things to yourself now when you make a mistake.

Practice being kind to yourself.

3. Know that this is a life-long process. We are going to slip and judge ourselves and others from time to time. When you catch yourself judging others—apologize. Tell them you're sorry. Tell them that you hated it when your father (or whomever it may have been) criticized you and that you didn't mean to do that to them. When you judge yourself, apologize to yourself and let go of the judgment.

It's a Choice

What we say to others and ourselves is a choice. Think of someone you respect—maybe it's a world leader, a famous author, or a spiritual figure. Choose a person who you know is an evolved soul and imagine what they would say and then say it to yourself. Think about what their perspective would be on whatever you are being critical about. For example, what would Mother Teresa say about your being angry because you failed an exam? She would probably hug you and tell you that you are loved whether you passed the exam or not.

Then, from that place of love, quiet your mind, study, and retake the test with a new perspective that you are not the result of a test.

You are changing your self-talk. The people who planted those original ideas that led to negative self-talk were wrong.

Notice. Practice. Allow the process.
Be patient and kind to yourself.

Once you've done that, apply this exercise when you are dealing with others, and your relationships will be more loving and fulfilling because people want to be accepted for who they are. When they make a mistake, they are usually so hard on themselves that they don't need you adding to their negative self-talk. They can do a great job of that on their own!

If you need to, speak your truth kindly, lovingly, and firmly. Avoid speaking to others from a critical place.

When you choose not to criticize yourself and others, you will have healthier, happier, more loving relationships, and you are a giant step closer to feeling fabulous forever.

5

The Costs of Being
a People Pleaser

I've known many people pleasers in my life, and I don't mind confessing to having been one in my past. What exactly is a people pleaser? It is someone who does things to make other people happy—to please them. That seems like a nice thing to do: to make others happy.

And that's not a bad thing, unless there's a cost to you. If you are doing something you don't want to do to please others, that's a problem. If you aren't speaking up to please others, that's a problem. If you aren't doing something you want to do to please others, that's also a problem. And those problems will come at a cost to you.

The Five Costs of Being a People Pleaser

1. Your spirit gets crushed.

2. Your heart doesn't get heard.

3. People will expect more and more—it will never be enough.

4. Your needs won't get met.

5. Your relationships will be imbalanced and unhealthy.

Those are significant costs. But the pain of those costs is usually not enough to get you to stop being a people pleaser. You know the costs in the back of your mind, even if you don't admit them to yourself.

It seems like it would be simple. Even if you're not a people pleaser yourself, you think that the pain of the costs would be enough to get people to stop pleasing others. But it's not quite that simple.

You see, there's a motive behind it; there's a payoff for people-pleasing behavior. It's not as altruistic as it sounds. I certainly don't want to make you or anybody else wrong, but until you know the payoff, you won't change the behavior and eliminate the costs. My goal is always to help you feel great about yourself!

In his fabulous book *Excuses Begone*, Wayne Dyer looks at eighteen of the main excuses people use to limit themselves and to not do what they say they want to do. He also takes it a step further and looks at the hidden payoffs, or perceived rewards, for those who use excuses. The truth is you won't stop using an excuse until you become aware of and change the payoff from using that excuse. The hidden payoffs Wayne Dyer says people get from their excuses are:

1. Avoidance

2. Safety

3. Taking the easy way out (lazy or getting others to do your work)

4. Manipulation

5. Being right

6. Blame

7. Protection

8. Escaping the present moment

Let's take the example of being a people pleaser and look at some of the possible payoffs for this behavior:

A mother might be a people pleaser when it comes to her teenage children. She lets them walk all over her and then complains that she doesn't have a life. She can't exercise or take classes because she has to take care of her children's "needs," such as cleaning up after them, doing their laundry, chauffeuring them and their friends around, and so on.

You and I can look at that and see that she needs to have better boundaries. She might use the excuse "there will be family drama" if she leaves her children for a few hours to start taking better care of herself. A possible payoff for this excuse is "avoidance" or "the easy way out" or "safety." It could be a combination of all three. In any case, she is afraid to make changes.

She won't change her behavior and give up her excuse until she replaces her payoff with something healthier or handles the fear of confrontation. If I were coaching her, I'd start by helping her get clarity on her payoffs and then look at what her fears really are as they relate to giving them up. Then little by little, we would replace that payoff with something else, such as the reward of being stronger and healthier, being around longer for her children, and setting a good example for her children.

Now let's look at how a people pleaser might function in a romantic relationship. I help women virtually every day deal with being a people pleaser when it comes to their partners.

Suppose a woman is in a committed relationship, and she is living with her boyfriend. He doesn't want her to go out with her friends. He feels jealous and threatened by them, and so little by little, she stops seeing her friends to please him.

When her friends complain that they never see her anymore, she comes up with excuses: "It's going to be too risky" or "I'm too scared to stand up to him because he might leave me" or "He gets so remote and withdrawn if I do go out with my friends that it's not worth the aggravation when I get home."

So what might be her payoff? "Avoidance" or "safety" or "the easy way out." But because I'm a coach, I would also look for a more deeply hidden payoff—"blame." She gets to blame her boyfriend and use him as an excuse to not go out with her friends. He looks manipulative, and her friends aren't going to like him. Maybe she would rather be with him than with her friends. But what if things don't work out? She can then say he was controlling. And she doesn't have to be responsible for not standing up to him. She can blame him for not respecting her feelings.

So you see, it can get quite complicated. But you can be

sure that if someone is using an excuse, there is a payoff. And until that payoff is replaced with something healthier and more honest, then it will dominate and the excuse mode will remain activated.

So if you know you're a people pleaser, look closely to see what your payoff is. Then replace the payoff with something positive.

Balance pleasing yourself with pleasing others. When you put yourself first, you will ultimately be happier, as well as more loving and giving. And that will please others who really care about you!

— 6 —

"Nice" Has Its Price!
Are You Too Nice?

There's a huge difference between being nice (pleasant) and being kind (caring). Many of us were raised to be nice girls. Any behavior that gets repeated long enough ultimately becomes a habit. In this case, being nice all the time becomes a habit that can keep you from speaking up for what you want and need. It can also create an opportunity for people to manipulate you. I teach my clients to replace the "nice girl" training with a new and more effective model of kindness. Why this is so important is that kindness, when combined with firmness, creates an effective way to live your life and communicate to others so that they can hear you.

At the 2007 Grammy Awards, "I'm Not Ready to Make Nice" by the Dixie Chicks won the Grammy for best song. Many people are familiar with the storm of controversy that spawned the creation of that song. In case you don't know, the Dixie Chicks, the hottest-selling female country band in music history, were knocked off a lot of radio stations and suffered significant financial damage when one of the band members expressed a controversial political viewpoint during a 2003 concert in London. It doesn't matter if you were "on their side" or not; what's most significant is that while they worked their way out of the controversy, they wrote their award-winning song; that can be a powerful guide for all of us. It's about not backing down no matter the cost to oneself and not caving in to pressure to do something other people think you should do.

The last line of the song, which is about not doing things simply to please others, is the key to living your life from a place of freedom, peace, and joy. If you live your life trying to please others and do what they think you should do, you will never be able to fulfill your own dreams and be happy.

You have to care more about how you feel than about what others think of you. If you don't, you'll always be at the mercy of others, doing things that don't feel good because you want them to like you or approve of you.

People will find all sorts of ways to try to manipulate you into doing things their way. They will give you gifts, promotions, raises, conditional "love," housing, food, and validation. They will act pouty, whiney, controlling, angry, or aloof to try to get you to do things their way. And all you have to do is give in, speak, act, and do it their way. All you have to do is sell your soul!

Am I being dramatic? Not really. When you live your life by someone else's standards and wishes, you aren't living it according to what feels fabulous for you. You will never be happy under those circumstances. And it's your life!

As women, many of us were raised to be seen and not heard to make sure we were perceived as being sweet and considerate. We were taught that being nice has benefits. After all, most of us had moms and dads who, to varying degrees, validated, rewarded, and loved us when we were good. And that might have been okay when we were small since we couldn't survive without Mom and Dad, but now as women, it's not healthy for us to be so focused on acting nice to please others.

I'm certainly not implying that you need to be nasty. Being both kind and firm is an appropriate and great guide for living your life, especially when you combine them with also being humble and loving. But if you think that you need people to like you more than you need to honor yourself, then you'll be stuck living your life the way others think you should.

The cost of being too nice, of pleasing others, is giving up your dreams, desires, choices, freedom, and joy of life. It might keep you from asking for a raise, taking a dream vacation, living in a favorite city, driving a fun car, having children, or getting an education—just to mention a few things you might sacrifice by being too nice and pleasing others.

Besides never making you happy, there's a bigger problem with the too-nice scenario. People who want you to do things their way and want you to make them happy don't really care about you. They only care about their own feelings and needs. They make terrible partners, friends, coworkers, and bosses. They care about themselves at your expense. And it's up to you to see the truth about them.

You will know if you're doing the nice-girl routine and they're taking advantage of you by not giving back equally.

You can tell when people are in the relationship for what they can get out of it when they don't put an equal amount into it. Are you always doing what they want to do, going to their favorite places, and generally doing it their way? If so, your partner doesn't really choose to care about you. If you stay, you will wake up one day and realize how unloved and empty you feel. You will realize that you don't know who you are, that you have lost yourself.

So do yourself a favor: find a partner, friend, or boss who also cares about you. Find someone who doesn't manipulate you with gifts, praise, supposed love, and other things to get their way. Find a partner who doesn't get pouty, whiney, controlling, angry, or aloof in an effort to manipulate you into doing things their way—especially when it is something you really don't want to do or know it is not good for you or it doesn't feel right for you.

As the Dixie Chicks learned, there is often a price to be paid for speaking your opinion, your truth. But the price of being too nice is far greater than any price you might pay for being true to yourself. Selling your soul to get material or other perceived gains isn't what you came here to do. You came here to live an authentic life. You came here to thrive. You can't thrive when you turn against yourself.

Choose to not back down. Choose to not make nice when it doesn't feel right. Choose to be kind, firm, humble, and loving. Choose to listen to your heart. Choose to trust that Divine Source/Creation has great people lined up for you if you make room for them. Then trust and stay positive!

7

Are Your Decisions Crushing Your Spirit?

The next time you have to make an important decision concerning your employment or a new job opportunity, a relationship, or even whether or not to accept a date, determine whether or not the decision you are leaning toward is based on fear or trust.

A fear-based decision is made to prevent something from happening that you're afraid of. A trust-based decision is made when you trust your heart and soul's voice to go where you are being called, knowing that the Universe will respond to that desire.

Here are some examples of how a fear-based decision might sound compared to a trust-based decision:

Fear-based: *I'd better take this job; they're offering me a lot of money and I might never get married, so I better be thinking of how to support myself in the future.*

Trust-based: *I'm grateful the company wants me, but I don't feel good about working there. They seem so cold and a little unprofessional. I'm going to hold out for a job where I can work hard, make a good living, and also have fun.*

Fear-based: *Why not date Tom? He's a successful, smart, and serious man. I know he wants me to dress up more than I like to, and he's kind of serious all the time, but I can manage that. And I don't know if someone as smart or successful will ask me out again.*

Trust-based: *It's so lovely that Tom wants to date me, but he's just not the kind of person I want to spend time with. I prefer men who are more relaxed and fun, where I can wear a T-shirt, shorts, and flip-flops on the weekend. I'm not going to date him. I'm going to wait to spend time with someone I'd rather be with.*

Why Do You Make Fear-Based Decisions?

You make fear-based decisions to get love, security, approval, or self-esteem from outside sources. And when you make a decision for the sake of security or approval or love, you often go against what your heart and soul truly desire. You go for the security because you don't trust that the Universe will send you something better. And you do it at a huge cost to yourself.

Oprah Winfrey is a perfect example of not choosing to make a decision for security. As I recall the story, when Oprah was very young, she was offered an anchor job that would have allowed her to earn $22,000 a year. Her father strongly advised her to take that job because it was safe. Fortunately for Oprah (and all of us) she turned it down and followed her heart.

Oprah is a clear example of the Universe powerfully responding when you choose to follow your heart's desire. Can you imagine what her life would have been like (not to mention the lives of the thousand of people she has helped along the way) if she had chosen security? She avoided a fear-based decision. (Thank you, Oprah!)

Other people make wrong choices in relationships because they are desperate for love. A woman might choose to marry a man she doesn't love. Her thinking is usually, "He loves me, he's a nice man, and even though I don't love him, at least I'm not alone."

More often than not, people make fear-based choices to get approval or to avoid disapproval. An example is deciding to buy an expensive outfit that you can't afford for a dinner party because you think your host will be impressed. That's performing for approval. Or you'll let people violate your work boundaries so they'll like you, keep you around, or maybe even promote you. Both have a high cost.

The Cost of Fear-Based Decisions

Making fear-based decisions to gain love, security, or self-esteem from the outside has a high cost attached to it. And it's too high a price to pay.

The cost is a crushed spirit!

If you make decisions that crush your spirit, you are crushing who you are: remember, you are a spiritual being having a human experience. So if you're not going to honor your spirit, you are essentially wasting your life. When you do this, you will end up depressed and wondering why it feels like your life has no meaning.

We all have the power of the Universe waiting to provide for us, to love us, and to protect us. All you have to do is trust it and receive its offerings. Oprah and successful people like her aren't any more special than you. People like that just trust their hearts and the Universe, they perform their work with passion and commitment, and they receive all the goodies the Universe has to offer. It has them for you too!

When you choose to give in to your fears to gain love, security, approval, or self-esteem, you're telling the Universe that you don't believe it will honor your heart's desires. And that is exactly what happens. The cost to your heart, soul, and overall well-being is huge!

Choose to honor your spirit and make trust-based decisions. Trust the Universe to bring you all the amazing goodies it has for you.

8

Perfection— The Prisoner of Your Soul!

Don't try to be perfect. The cost of perfection is too high. It exhausts your supply of joy, fun, humor, growth, learning, freedom, love, and loving relationships. And don't expect perfection from others. There's an Italian proverb that goes like this: "He that will have a perfect brother must resign himself to remain brotherless." In other words, nobody's perfect. But that doesn't mean people won't try.

Even I'm no stranger to trying to be perfect. I had to learn to say, "I've done my best." That is the only way to ultimately overcome trying to be perfect—accepting that you've done your best and saying to yourself, "I've done my best" and then stop working. Close up the computer, turn in the paper, give the okay to the graphic designer. . . .

The problem with trying to be perfect is that it's exhausting to you and others if they're also working on the project. A lot of times when people see you trying to be perfect, it makes them uncomfortable, and often they'll withdraw or run. And guess what: the minute you try to be perfect around someone, that's when you'll make a mistake. We've all done it. What's most important, though, is that it's only a mistake if you're trying to be perfect. If you are just being yourself—human, vulnerable, full of emotions, fears, and challenges; dealing with family, career, financial, or health issues; full of love, hope, and expectations—you *will* make mistakes.

The good news is you usually learn from your mistakes. If you get cranky with someone because they weren't perfect, they will probably withdraw, and you will need to apologize. That's no big deal—you will just have to make amends.

Let's face it: you are going to have good days and bad days. You are going to unintentionally say the wrong thing to someone, accidentally cut someone off on the road, misunderstand what someone said to you, or be too tired to ask for clarification.

It's how you go about making amends, or cleaning up the mess, that makes the difference. And if a mistake costs you a relationship, then perhaps that is not a relationship you really wanted to be in. Can you imagine a lifetime of being afraid to make mistakes in your relationships?

The need to be perfect usually comes from trying to please a critical parent, teacher, older sibling, lover, or spouse. Those people were probably raised by perfectionists themselves. They think you need to be perfect, and if you're not, they think it's a negative reflection on them. They will attempt and often succeed in shaming you. And once you accept that shame, you are trapped in the pain and rigidity of the perfectionist model. Rebel and throw off that shame. Don't let anyone give you something you can't benefit from. It's their issue; don't make it yours.

In the perfection model, there isn't any room for creativity, growth, learning, or forgiveness. Perfection brings with it tension, constriction, anger, withdrawal, and rebellion, as well as the killer of so many relationships: no space for forgiveness.

Not being perfect doesn't mean you don't strive for excellence. In the excellence model, there *is* room for creativity, growth, learning, freedom, mistakes, forgiveness, and fun! There is heart in this model. You are striving to do your best, to excel at something. It stretches you beyond where you thought you could go. And if you make a mistake—oh, well, try again.

Have you ever watched a dancer with "perfect" moves? He or she looks good, but there is something missing. The dancer isn't feeling the music or having a good time. They are too concerned with trying to be perfect, and it shows in the performance.

The best example of this I can recall occurred during the 1994 Winter Olympic Games in Lillehammer. Nancy Kerrigan and Oksana Baiul competed for the Gold Medal in figure skating. Nancy's performance was technically perfect, but it obviously lacked heart and tenderness.

On the other hand, Oksana (a sixteen-year-old girl who had endured much misfortune but still had her faith) skated beyond perfection—with heart, soul, love, and beauty. It still brings tears to my eyes to remember her flawless, heartfelt, breathtakingly beautiful performance.

Nancy Kerrigan was outraged that she had lost the gold. She had been perfect. But that was the problem. She had been technically perfect, but she hadn't shared her heart and soul with the audience, as Oksana had. Oksana brought her heart and soul to the competition, gave them to the audience, and won the gold.

Your heart and soul are already perfect. It is only your mind that thinks your behavior needs to be perfect. If you choose to "do your best" and express yourself from your heart and soul, others will feel your love, compassion, truthfulness, and openness, and they are more likely to lovingly respond and trust you. And since they are "imperfect" too, they will feel safer and more courageous with you.

If you live from your mind and always try to be perfect, you become rigid and send off a vibe that says, "I'm not soft and loving." It is difficult to attract a partner with that attitude.

Your spirit will be squelched in the perfection model. You won't be able to breathe, create, or fly. You'll be caged and stuck in a prison of perfection—alone, or worse, with another perfectionist!

So the choice is yours. Think about how it feels to try to be perfect. Feel where your body and heart constrict, then choose to let that go and be yourself. Let your perfect heart and soul lead you in life. Let your spirit fly free. Do your best.

One of the greatest dancers of all time, Martha Graham, noted, "You see, when weaving a blanket, an Indian woman leaves a flaw in the weaving of that blanket to let the soul out."

Don't let your soul be imprisoned by your mind's insistence on perfection. Tell your mind to be quiet, feel the music, move, and love! The gold is yours—given to you, by you, just for being the perfectly imperfect you.

9

Are You Creating Joy or Drama?

We create our lives either deliberately or by default. We either make decisions or decisions get made for us. What is it that you want to create in your life and in your relationships? What are your relationships like right now? Know that they are mirroring your thoughts. It might not be what you consciously want to create, but it is what you are creating subconsciously. So let's bring the truth to the surface so you can change it to what you want it to be.

There are some people who pursue a life filled with drama. After all, drama is rich and deep, but it is also ultimately exhausting and boring, not only to you but also to others. However, most of us simply don't know how to change our situations so that there is less drama and more joy.

All you have to do is watch a soap opera and you'll know what I mean by drama. Often, the scripts are written for most of the characters to be, among other things, either jealous, threatening, unhappy, backstabbing, cheating, lying, manipulating, always crying, or being distraught. It's always over the top, but I've known and seen a lot of people who live their lives that way—maybe not every day, but too often to experience the joy and fun of life.

If soap operas are the extreme end of the drama scale, what does the other end look like, the people who live their lives in drama? Well, they worry incessantly, they get anxious when things don't go the way they planned, and they expect things to fall apart. They call their friends and family and talk about whatever is going on for hours at a time. Even the smallest things are a big deal. They blow everything out of proportion. They don't have a sense of, *This will all work out. Sure it might take some effort, but I'll figure it out, after all this is a loving, supportive Universe, and it'll be fine. I just need to surrender and be guided to a solution.*

How to Change From a Life of Drama to One of Joy

First, you want to realize that you live in a supportive Universe with a loving, beneficent Divine Source who always has your back. There are always solutions to problems, and you aren't alone. Ever. Ask and you will receive whatever you need—a solution, a friend, a therapist, an editor, a banker, an idea, and so on. Anything and everything is possible and is there for you.

Second, assume positive intentions from others. This is the secret of happy, productive, and fun-loving people. Most humans mean to do the right thing; they are good, caring people. Everyone makes mistakes, though, and makes a mess at times as well. Allow people to clean up their messes and assume they meant to do the right thing.

Third, set an intention—one that will also be meaningful for you. If you are ready for joy, start by envisioning your life the way you want it to be. Think of all the positive things in your life, about all of the things that *have* gone your way.

Do you want to have a joyful, fun-loving relationship with someone who respects you, has integrity, honors their commitments, and honors your boundaries? Ask yourself "Why?" and answer honestly. Why do you want this relationship? Knowing the answer to this question is a crucial step in bringing this relationship into creation. The *why* adds the richness and depth to what you want. It paints the picture with all the colors, texture, and depth.

Now look to see if you have any doubts or negative thoughts. Those negative thoughts or doubts will block the flow of what you want. So if you think that you can't have a relationship without drama, examine why you think you need drama. What does the drama give you?

Most of us who had or have drama in our lives were victims of someone early on. That was our real drama. We were young and innocent and someone took that innocence away from us. We had to survive and we lived with drama, and it became familiar. But as you heal from that through coaching, counseling, and/or spirituality, you can move past the drama in your relationships.

It's impossible to eliminate all drama from your life. I just want you to focus on joy. Having drama in your life isn't bad. There are lots of appropriate and healthy ways to experience the high energy associated with drama. For instance, you can volunteer to work with homeless people. Or go to a children's hospital and participate in programs for children who are battling life-threatening or debilitating diseases or conditions. Or spend time at a nursing home with those who do not have visitors. Homeless people, sick people, elderly people—they have real drama, and if you like drama, volunteering to help these people may be just what you need.

When you remove the drama from your relationships, you are free to create joy in them.

Now It Is Time to Create Joy

How? Choose it! Start by bringing joyful thoughts into your mind. Consciously appreciate all the things in your life, even the little things. Think about the many blessings you already have.

Write down all the positive things in your life. Start with a blank notebook and set aside a page for each topic. Write down all the positive things about your home, work, love life, family, friendships, and health. Read it and add to it daily.

You create from the positive, not from the negative. Focusing on the negative only gets you more negative. So focus only on the positive! Instead of reading the news, start your day by reading a powerful spiritual book. (See the Recommended Reading section on page 159.) Do your morning ritual with tea or coffee and peaceful music, and enjoy the beginning of the day. Set an intention to experience joy each day. Choose joy! Meditate to quiet your mind.

Choose to love yourself unconditionally. When you notice

that you are criticizing or getting angry with yourself, stop. Be loving instead. Remember you are always growing.

Another aspect of joy is compassion. Be compassionate. The more compassionate you feel toward yourself and others, the more joy you will feel. As you begin to master unconditional love and compassion, you will feel joy. Feel it moment to moment. That's how joy works. It comes from being, not doing.

We are here to feel joy. From that joyful place, we are uplifted and we have the ability to positively impact a vast number of people. Start by choosing joy and uplifting yourself and those around you.

Assume positive intentions from other's words and behavior. Set an intention to experience joy every day, and then choose it minute by minute to live the kind of life you were meant to live—a joyful, loving, creative, and inspiring life.

❦ 10 ❦
Are You Healing or Hiding?

Opportunities for healing can come to us in the least expected ways. A few years ago, I had a truly wonderful vacation with my husband at a lovely resort on the Caribbean side of Mexico. I love the Mexican people because they are heart-centered. And I love the beauty of the water, which is restorative and healing. How interesting that I would be in a healing place.

Even while we're on vacation, our souls, in their infinite wisdom, provide us with opportunities for healing. This is true no matter where we are. Here's an example:

As I was checking in at Los Angeles International Airport, the wheels on my suitcase hit the base of a security sign. I tripped and fell backward and landed smack on my back. Fortunately, I was okay—just a little bruised and misaligned. The real pain was the fear that got temporarily activated. This was not how I expected to start my vacation. I had to do some quick work to keep that fear from ruining it. The fall became an opportunity for deeper healing, and, as a result, I really rested, relaxed, and healed on my vacation.

I'm sharing this because we've all had pain in our lives, especially in our relationships. And when our fear gets activated, we tend to withdraw to protect ourselves. It's as natural as breathing.

Childhood wounds give us lots of healing practice. As you'll read in the author's note at the back of this book, I experienced some trauma as a child. Because of all the work I've done to heal from my childhood wounds, I know that when fear gets activated within me, I need to immediately seek ways to heal rather than withdrawing to protect myself.

What's wrong with withdrawal? In the beginning, nothing is wrong with it. It all depends on how long you stay withdrawn. If you stay withdrawn for too long, you're essentially hiding, and then you're not living, loving, exploring, or experiencing life. And you aren't taking the final steps necessary for healing.

Healing is a step-by-step process. We take care of ourselves, we soothe our hearts, we learn to forgive and love again, and then move forward, baby step by baby step. How do we know when we're ready?

I used to fall a lot. My balance wasn't the best, and I would always rush and not pay attention to where I was going. For me, after a fall, it would take a little time—maybe a few days or a week—before I felt strong, centered, and stable on my feet again. I'd get massages, chiropractic adjustments, osteopathic treatments, and work with my coach. My icepack was my friend, and moving slowly became more my speed (not entirely a bad thing). I'm taking good care of myself now. I practice what I call mindful walking. And I remember my connection to Divine Source, who loves and protects me. (After all, I did have a great vacation, fall or no fall.)

Healing from a bad or painful relationship requires the same faith, self-care, and help from trained professionals. If you've ended a long-term relationship or lost someone close to you, doing some psychotherapy, hypnotherapy, coaching, or some other healing form of work to understand and honor your feelings is vitally important to your healing process. Doing spiritual work is a necessity. (See the Recommended Reading section on page 159 for some wonderful book suggestions to help you along the way.)

You will want to give yourself time to feel like you can walk without falling and hurting yourself, or be in a relationship without getting bruised again. A year is usually a good amount of time after the end of a significant relationship to work through a lot of the pain and sadness so that you can trust yourself to be in the dating world again.

Learning to feel steady on your feet in the world of relationships is learning to trust your emotions—for example, *I feel good when I'm with this person; I don't feel good when I'm with that person.* It is learning to know what works and what doesn't work for you. It is learning to honor and enforce your boundaries. When you can do those things, then you will feel safe about beginning a new relationship.

But how much time is too much time? What is the difference between withdrawing to avoid getting hurt and taking time to heal? There isn't a formula, but there are some basic guidelines.

If you hear yourself saying negative things about dating, then you know you are trying to protect yourself. If you notice that you are purposely avoiding social events, again you are trying to protect yourself. If you date someone who turns out not to be what you are looking for and so you go back into hiding, you are also trying to protect yourself.

Don't get me wrong: there's nothing wrong with trying to protect yourself. I'm just encouraging you *not* to go into hiding. Instead, use your awareness, your boundaries, and Divine Source to protect you. Allow your previous experiences to help you determine whether or not someone's behavior is working for you. For instance, if you value being on time and you used to become upset when your ex-boyfriend was always late to functions and now you are dating someone who is also always late, that person's behavior isn't going to work for you. Or, if you are financially responsible and your previous husband wasn't and it created a lot of challenges for you, then go the other way if you meet another man who is financially irresponsible. You know what behavior didn't work for you in the past. Don't try to go down that path again. It always ends in heartbreak, and maybe even bad credit, among other unfortunate things.

Ultimately, after you've been hurt, you will need to get back out into the world to get centered and stable, and to feel good about life again. If I never went anywhere ever again to protect myself from falling and getting hurt, I would have prevented myself from healing.

The ultimate healing comes when you're back in the world. It's about getting back on your feet, going out on dates or attending social gatherings, and surviving them. And you know what? It's okay if you fall down again. You'll learn to take even better care of yourself.

One more important thing: You are connected to a powerful, loving Divine Source who wants to shower you with love, joy, and abundance and is always with you, whether you realize it or not.

The day I fell in the airport, my husband was on one side, and out of nowhere appeared a kind man to ask if he could help me up. I realized a little later that he was an angel who had touched my back to heal my pain and fear. I had my precious husband on one side and an angel on the other. I am loved. Divine Source does help us when we fall or get hurt. We aren't alone, and we aren't supposed to be.

Put your hand on your heart and breathe in Divine Source's love for you.

This is a loving, supportive Universe. You are loved and watched over by an all-loving, all-powerful Divine Source. Choose to know you are connected to that love. Choose to feel that love. Choose to trust Divine Source and your own footing and get back into the world. There is an angel waiting for you to guide your way.

— 11 —

Do You Perform for Love?
Do You Expect Others
to Perform for Yours?

Performing for love never works. Yet we often think that if we do something a certain way or say something in particular or don't say something that we will keep another person loving us. We also might think that a person we love has to behave a certain way for us to continue loving them. They may feel like they have to walk, talk, dress, work, and clean a certain way and then we'll love them. Do you create that scenario in any of your relationships?

This is the sort of conditional love many of us felt as children. We became conditioned to believe that certain behavior earned us our parents' love and certain other types of behavior earned us their dislike or anger. So we've carried this forward into our present. But this doesn't work for us, does it?

What do you want instead? What does everyone want instead? I found the answer in an e-zine I received from a lovely man, Lee Glickstein. He used this quote in the e-zine, and I am unable to locate an attribution. However, I'm sure that whoever the author is, he or she will approve of my using it here to share with you.

> What we needed (as children) in large doses were receptive eyes, soft gazes signifying: "I am here for you. I see you, I hear you. There is nothing to do, nothing to perform. You don't have to smile or delight me to keep me here. Just being with you and breathing together is my great pleasure."
>
> —AUTHOR UNKNOWN

Wow, when I read that quote, tears welled up in my eyes. I could feel my heart softening and I could hear the little girl and the woman in me saying, *Yes, that's what I want, what I've always wanted. And it's how I want to make others feel when they're with me.*

Take this opportunity to fully be with that quote and live it, both for yourself and others. Give yourself the respect and love that come with realizing you don't have to perform or smile or delight yourself. You just get to be. And extend that same beauty and love to all the others in your life. That goes for the person who pushes your buttons the most. The person who you say you dislike. Just see them and breathe with them.

People are starving for that level of acceptance. That's why when they experience it from another person, they want that person to be with them all the time. But then that can become the same as asking someone to perform for your love so that you can feel good. Instead, just accept them in return. Give your unconditional acceptance to three people today, and most important, give it to yourself.

Choose to be here for yourself. Choose to not have to perform. Choose to love and let everyone just be. Choose to be with them and yourself and breathe together.

—⁂ 12 ⁂—

Six Common Mistakes Women Make in Relationships and How to Correct Them

Let's look at the common mistakes many women make that can keep them from having truly fantastic relationships. Then, in case you are making those same mistakes yourself, I'll offer you suggestions on how to turn them around. Don't be too alarmed if any of these apply to you. You can easily change them, usually just by realizing what they are and what you can do instead. Here they are:

1 **Not saying no, defining boundaries, and sticking to them.** For example, maybe you have trouble saying no to your boss who wants you to work late. You've told him before that you can't work late, but you've caved in and stayed, so now he doesn't listen to you when you say you can't stay late. Or maybe you have trouble saying no to your boyfriend who doesn't want you to go out with your friends You want to be with your friends, and you've told him you're going out with them tomorrow night, but he starts giving you the silent treatment tonight, so you give in and don't go. (You don't want him pouting—or worse, breaking up with you.) Or maybe you have difficulty saying no to a friend who wants to cry on your shoulder when it's your gym night—again. Each time she does this, you tell yourself it's the last time, but each time you give in and listen to her, and by then, it's too late to go to the gym.

2 **Being too nice despite the price.** Women who are too nice often don't want to offend anyone, so they don't let people know how they're feeling. Also, women don't like things to be messy, so they tend to want to clean up things or people. It's important to realize that you can't always clean up other people's messes. Life isn't always about being neat and tidy.

3 **Settling for crumbs in a romantic relationship—or settling for "good enough."** For example, you're with a man you like who is kind and sort of fun, but you know something is missing in your relationship. He's good, but not great for you. "Great for you" includes a kind, likeable, and fun-loving man with whom you also feel the joy and the passion that accompany love and a connection that transcends the physical.

4 **Not giving yourself permission to be spicy, saucy, and hot!** You've probably been around women who never strut their stuff. Sometimes you want to put on a pair of high heels, wear a nice-fitting sweater and skirt, put on your favorite earrings, dab on some perfume, and go out and have fun and kick your heels up on a dance floor. It doesn't matter if you can dance or not. Have fun. Being spicy, saucy, and hot isn't about wearing your blouse open down to your navel; it's about feeling that way internally and taking that out into the world from time to time. We don't want to end up being angry and resentful of other women who are more out there than we are.

5 **Taking things personally and reacting to what people say or do and feeling bad about it.** If a person is mean, nasty, rude, aloof, angry, or critical, you might think that you caused that behavior. That often leads to feelings of unworthiness. You may think that if someone treated you that way, you must deserve it.

6 **Letting negative self-talk convince you that you aren't desirable.** If you think you aren't desirable, you won't be. So either you'll attract someone who thinks you aren't desirable, or no one at all.

What Women Can Do Instead . . .

1 **Learn to say no when necessary and mean it.** Get clear about what works and doesn't work for you; let people know and then stick to it. When you draw a boundary and hold it, you're teaching people that you mean what you say. If you don't hold to it, then you're teaching them that they can talk you into doing what they want you to do. They will keep after you until you give in.

2 **Stop being too nice.** Being nice has its place, of course, but people often read "too nice" behavior as if you really don't mean what you're saying or that you're a pushover. They will think they can talk you into doing things their way. So if your boss wants you to work late even though you have plans and you are too nice about saying no instead of being firm, then he or she might read that as you can be talked into working late. And if you're invested in being too nice, you'll give in, cancel your plans, and work late. (Keep in mind, though, that I'm not suggesting you be mean to your boss. You can still be kind without being too nice. Kind is effective and necessary. Nice can be manipulated.)

The same concepts apply to boyfriends, husbands, or children. If you tell people kindly and firmly that you have other plans and cannot do what they are asking of you, they will be fine. If they get pouty, they're just trying to manipulate you into staying home with them. Ignore their pouty behavior.

Children will often try to get away with not picking up their things, not doing their chores, and/or avoiding their homework. If you're kind and firm and have solid boundaries, they will know you mean business and will eventually back down. Life becomes so much easier when you stand your ground.

3 **Realize that you don't have to settle for good enough.** You *can* have "great." I see so many women settling for situations that don't really meet their needs. For instance, you might convince yourself that you could be alone the rest of your life, so you better be with this "good" man. Instead, what you want to do is write a list of your ideal partner's qualities, traits, and characteristics. Use all of your past experiences and turn any negatives into positives. For example, if you know you want a man who doesn't drink too much, you can add "occasionally enjoys a few drinks on the weekend" to your list. Once you have your list, read it every day and daydream for fifteen minutes about being in a relationship with this wonderful person. It works. If you compile the list and spend time daydreaming, while at the same time you don't allow any negative thoughts to block him from coming to you and you connect to Divine Source, it *will* happen.

4 **Get back in touch with the part of yourself that is spicy, saucy, and hot.** When you are in touch with your spicy, saucy, and hot qualities, you will feel great about yourself and have more fun. Jeannie Cheatham, an eighty-year-old blues singer and pianist, is my role model. The last time I saw her, she was as spicy, saucy, and hot as they come. You will feel so alive when you get back in touch with this energy. Put on a red dress, listen to some great sassy music, go dancing, start singing, do whatever works for you. Just let it rip! (For more about Jeannie, see page 105.)

5 **Learn not to take things personally.** The truth is nothing anyone does is personal. It's *never* about you. It's *always* about them. When you learn this basic truth, you will be freer and will have more fun and energy. In his bestselling book *The Power of Intention,* Wayne Dyer talks about not being offended. It's only the ego that gets offended. If you don't take things personally, you won't get offended. You won't get hurt or angry. You won't waste precious time and energy being hurt or angry. Life will inevitably bring most of us things that will hurt and make us angry. Save your energy for those unavoidable situations.

Remember that people say and do things because of their own wounds. So if someone is nasty, it's because of something inside of them that hurts and is causing them to lash out. It's not about you. Get out of their energy field, and you won't need to experience their negative energy. If it's a boss, then just realize, "Oh well, that's just the way she or he is. It has nothing to do with me." Try it and see what you notice. It works.

6 **Stop saying negative things about yourself.** Many women do this all the time. And it's the single-most destructive thing you can do.

You have a choice to think positive things about yourself or negative things. Let me say that again: YOU HAVE A CHOICE ABOUT WHAT TO THINK!

If you've had a lot of practice thinking negative things, it's going to take a little time to change the negative to the positive. But it doesn't have to take long. It's a matter of paying attention to what your mind (ego) is saying and choosing not to listen to it. Change it to something positive.

If you think you aren't desirable, you won't be desirable. You won't have the romantic relationship you want. Or if you're in a relationship and you don't feel desirable, that relationship won't be fulfilling and exciting; you'll have attracted someone who ends up thinking you're not desirable. Your thoughts create your reality.

So instead of making negative comments about your nose, legs, stomach, intelligence, or education, focus on the good things about you. If you can't think of any, ask a friend, parent, coworker, or sibling. Listen and then choose to believe them.

YOU HAVE A CHOICE! You can think positively or negatively about yourself. It's nothing more than a choice.

You can say no, set boundaries, and be kind and firm instead of "nice." You can choose to create and attract a great man. You can choose to be spicy, saucy, and hot. You can choose to not take things personally. And you can choose to think positive things about yourself.

You can have the life you dream of and deeply desire! You are a child of Divine Source, and thus you are precious, important, and loved. And everything you ask for will be given to you if you just keep believing.

─๑ 13 ๑─

Were You Really Betrayed?

One of my core teachings is that no matter what someone does or doesn't do, it's never personal. If a person yells at you, manipulates you, talks down to you, is rude or unfriendly to you, or even if they are sweet to you, it *always* has to do with them. It has nothing to do with you. That's why it's not personal to you. It's their behavior. It comes from their minds and their hearts. If it's unkind, it comes from *their* wounds. If it's kind, it comes from *their* hearts.

After people coach with me, they truly grasp this concept. They know it's true. As a result, their lives change for the better. They relax and learn to live a more joyful and peaceful life.

There is one area where this concept is challenging to apply, and that's when a person feels betrayed by their significant other. If you are in a committed serious relationship with a person who has an affair with someone else, it feels awful and devastating. Your trust is shattered. Your idea of what you thought you had with that person is destroyed. The trust and the relationship can be rebuilt, but not if you take it personally.

It's not personal. If your significant other chose to be with someone else, it had nothing to do with you. It was all about him or her. It was something that person needed, wanted, desired, and chose. Of course you might not want to be with someone who made that choice, and that's *your* choice to make.

An Unhealthy Reaction

It is normal to feel upset in a situation like that, of course. However, the problem arises when a person who has been deceived remains angry and stays that way for years. Holding on to that anger magnifies the supposed betrayal and keeps it stuck in your mind. To what end?

Women will say they don't trust men. When I ask why, they inevitably tell me they've been "cheated" on. That's a loaded word. It makes you feel awful about yourself. With venom and anger in their voices, they tell me what *he* did. The hate and anger pouring out of their hearts are palpable.

It's honest to be mad at first. And it's how you move yourself out of despair and rejection. But staying mad isn't healthy. It keeps you stuck in negative energy.

A Healthy Response

If that happened to you, what if instead you said, "Well, he chose to be with another woman and didn't tell me. It really hurt me and made me sad. He even lied about where he was at times. I don't trust him anymore. I decided he isn't the man for me. I know it's not personal; it's about him. And it's not okay with me. He obviously has some things to work out. I'm moving on." Then, you are free to move on and seek out a relationship with someone who has worked through their wounds so they won't act out in this manner.

A Freeing Choice

What if your partner apologizes and wants to stay in the marriage or relationship? What do you do then? You will then decide if you think the relationship is worth saving. If so, your partner will need to work to regain your trust, and at the same time, you need to forgive him. It's a whole lot easier to forgive someone if you don't take it personally. And since it's not personal, when a person goes off with someone else, then doesn't that make forgiveness a healthy choice?

Remember, forgiveness isn't about condoning behavior; it's "for giving love to yourself and someone else." If you really love this person and you're willing to accept that their behavior had nothing to do with you, that they were trying to heal an old wound or learn something about themselves, then the next logical step is forgiveness for their actions.

How to Not Feel Betrayed

I'm not saying it's easy to forgive, but you need to make it as easy on yourself as possible. For instance, don't let your mind wonder what she looks like, what she has that you don't have, what made her so special that he was willing to risk the relationship to be with her, or whatever other thoughts your mind can conjure up.

Don't go there because it isn't relevant. He went there for his own reasons. It has nothing to do with you or with her. It's about him. Trying to understand why he did what he did doesn't help. It actually keeps you stuck in a negative energy field.

Your key to freedom from feeling devastated, betrayed, cheated on, or rejected is to not take it personally. It isn't personal. Again, it was about him. You might think that the two of you are linked or that together you make one, and so to think that it didn't have anything to do with you might make you even angrier. But the truth is, you are separate people. You are individuals. So you need to think like an individual.

Be true to yourself. Love yourself. He made his decision. Now you make yours. What decision serves you? What's the healthy choice for you? To come up with your truth, move into your heart. Get out of your head. Don't listen to your ego, your critical voice. Listen to your heart. What does it want to do?

If your spouse had an affair years ago and you are still angry or bitter about it, what do you need to do right now to finally let the anger and bitterness go? At this point, it's just an excuse to keep you from having a relationship. Your spouse didn't reject *you*. Rather, he did something for himself. And that's when you knew he wasn't the guy you wanted to be with. Finally, let him go by letting go of taking it personally. Make a healthier choice.

Virtually nothing is more unattractive than a bitter, resentful woman. And it's a cowardly excuse for not being vulnerable. And worst of all, it's keeping you from love. You don't have to attract another man who will be unfaithful. But if you focus on it, you will. So move on. Take a risk. Go for love. Stop taking everything personally. It's not about you.

Choose to let go. Choose to love again. Choose to be free from your critical mind. Choose to allow glorious love into your heart and life.

⚛ 14 ⚛

Rejection—Is It Real?

Rejection feels real, even though it rarely is. To understand this, let's take a look at what rejection is: It looks or feels like someone has decided they don't want anything to do with you. They don't want to spend time, money, or share their heart with you. This person has seemingly rejected you in favor of someone or something else. Or so it seems at first glance. What makes rejection hurt so much is that you perceive it to be a rejection of you as a person, a human being.

The dictionary definition of rejection is "to discard as defective or useless." That zings right into our hearts, and we take it personally. We think we are unworthy.

One thing I know for certain is that absolutely no one on this earth can truthfully say to you that you're defective or useless. If someone says this to you, you can reject their comment for the untruth that it is. It's a lie.

It's a Lie!

You aren't defective, flawed, or useless. No one is. As long as you are breathing, you have an opportunity to be quite useful, and if there is something you want to change about your life, you can do that.

Why do you think that the other person's behavior, words, or thoughts are about you? They aren't. Remember, it's about them. Always. It's about what works and doesn't work for them. And if you don't work, match, or fit for someone, I guarantee you that you will work, match, or fit for someone else. And someone else will work better for you. And if someone can make you feel defective or useless, then underneath, you feel that way; otherwise, you would reject that thought.

You aren't defective. You aren't useless. You're a Goddess. Be one. Carry yourself as one. Act as if you are a Goddess until you fully believe it and honor it.

I worked with a fabulous woman who I will call Teresa. She is smart, kind, funny, and very upbeat. But every time a man didn't want to be with her, she felt rejected. And it would put her into a tailspin. She'd feel like she'd never meet a man who would like her for herself. Unfortunately, then no man would come near her, because that was the energy she was putting out into the world—*You really won't want to come near me, I'm defective.* Of course, that wasn't what she meant to do.

The way life works is that you get what you think about, whether you want it or not. So if you're thinking that someone might or will reject you—that's exactly what will happen.

Teresa understood the concept of attracting what you think about. She and I worked on having her realize and focus on the things that she liked about herself. As she did that daily for a couple of months, she began to shift.

Step by step, she began to realize she wasn't defective and that she was useful and so much more. She realized she was attractive, fun, smart, funny, and discriminating. She didn't want just any man. She wanted a wonderful, kind, smart, funny, responsible, loving, passionate, healthy man.

When we looked at the various men who had been in her life and what had been going on with them, she realized they weren't a good fit for the new, authentic Teresa. She looked closely and realized they weren't rejecting her. It wasn't personal.

They had their own issues, insecurities, fears, and so on. She quickly saw that she was better off without them in her life. They didn't work for her! Neither person was defective or useless; they just weren't meant to be together in a romantic way. Teresa is now dating and enjoying herself and holding herself in high esteem.

Another client, whom I'll call Sarah, wrote the following to me in an e-mail: "My boyfriend just broke up with me, and I'm feeling so rejected. I know I shouldn't, but I can't help it. Can you give me some insights so that I don't have to feel bad about myself?"

This is how I responded:

I know from reading your full e-mail to me that the reason he broke up with you is that he wasn't ready for a long-term committed relationship, and you are.

So think of it this way: he wasn't rejecting you as a person; he was saying that what you wanted wasn't what he wanted right now. He is extremely busy, at age 33, building his career and proving to himself that he can be successful. That is his choice. It doesn't seem to have anything to do with you.

Sarah, he isn't rejecting you; he is choosing his priorities. And career and success are his priorities. Not a relationship.

Keep staying open. Honor your choice and his choice. It's not personal. He has a right to his choices. And remember you are a Goddess, and the best man will come into your life. Someone who is ready for a commitment. By letting him go, you are opening the space both in your heart and energetically for the best man.

So please keep working on yourself and keep your heart open. That way, the man you are meant to be with can find you, and then the committed relationship you want will be right for both of you.

You are on the right track. Keep looking and loving.

The *Best* Relationship

When you are in the best relationship for yourself and for the other person, you'll know it. It doesn't mean you are home free. There is always work in relationships. But that person, the best person for you, doesn't make you feel rejected when he has to take care of his own business. You know he loves you. He tells you in different ways. He shows his feelings for you. And you show him love and appreciation, which creates a safe and courageous space for him, and that makes a man really happy and a good partner.

Heal Your Heart

If feeling rejected is a recurring theme in your life, then start right now to change it. Begin by listing all the wonderful qualities you have. Then ask friends and family what it is they appreciate and like about you. Then look back on past relationships and honestly ask yourself where the man was in his life when he stopped being with you. (Don't use the word "rejection.") What was going on in his life? What kind of man was he really?

Often we love someone and know they are truly a good person, but their behavior is awful. Or maybe they just aren't available, so they can't be in a relationship. Maybe they came from an abusive home, and they don't know how to love or how to communicate.

Look honestly, and then answer this question: Were they rejecting me or were they unable to be in a relationship with a Goddess like me?

What I notice is the majority of women know the man wasn't a good fit; they were just afraid of being alone and so they settled. That's another book, but look and ask yourself honestly if you were settling. You don't have to, so don't. And the man who is right for you will love you to pieces.

Your Choice

It's your choice whether you choose to feel rejected or to accept that someone wasn't the best person for you, or vice versa. There isn't anything wrong in either case. No one is wrong, defective, or useless. You just weren't a good fit for each other. So don't feel bad about yourself. You're a Goddess!

*Love yourself, see your goodness, honor your
Goddess, and remember, you are fabulous!*

PART TWO

What Works to Feel Fabulous Now and Forever!

In this part, I'm going to share with you the things you need to do to truly feel fabulous and ideas for how to live in that place for the rest of your life. This isn't about feeling it for a month or for a year; it's about feeling fabulous *forever*. You'll want to start incorporating some of these recommendations and suggestions into your life on a daily, weekly, or monthly basis; other recommendations and suggestions can be tried on for size when you need to shift a limiting perspective—painful or otherwise—that is no longer serving you or when the ego (that gremlin!) gets reactivated. Other ideas I share in this part require some lifestyle modifications and choices that will help you choose to feel fabulous forever!

— 15 —

Start Feeling Fabulous Now!

I want to share a little story of a woman who was close to feeling fabulous, but she just couldn't own it. One New Year's Eve, my husband and I went to a wonderful restaurant. While we were waiting to be seated, I noticed the couple waiting behind us. The woman had on a stunning dress. Never one to withhold a compliment from my sister Goddesses, I turned to her and said, "That's a gorgeous dress. You look fabulous!"

She looked at me and said, "He made me wear it," and pointed to her date. I was stunned for a moment. As you can imagine, the coach in me wanted to start coaching her immediately. Of course I didn't. I smiled and said something to try to help her feel a little more comfortable about wearing such a beautiful dress.

If you are going to go to all the trouble to dress up and put on an amazing dress and someone compliments you—accept it. It's one important way you let yourself feel fabulous.

As my brother-in-law said, "When a woman doesn't accept a man's compliments, he stops giving them."

We don't want people to stop complimenting us. So smile, be gracious, and say thank you. People will love you for it. And you'll keep getting compliments.

A woman who exemplifies feeling fabulous is Kate Middleton. We know her as the woman who came from a middle-class family—her parents were both originally air stewards—and married Prince William in 2011 to become Her Royal Highness, The Duchess of Cambridge. It is a modern-day fairytale.

The fact that she married a prince and became a princess is a delight. But it's not the fact that she became a princess that drew my attention to her; it's the way she moves in the world. She seems comfortable in her own skin, likes to have fun, wears clothes that look fabulous on her, and is gracious and kind. You can see people positively respond to her easygoing demeanor.

As I watched her wave to the crowd after her wedding, I could see her ease shining through. She was having a good time. She didn't have that stiff royal wave; rather, she waved normally like anyone would. She and Prince William had dated during college, but, as the news stories report, he broke up with her to date other women, many from wealthier and titled families. Ultimately, Prince William came back to Kate, a woman who seems to share his values, comes from a hardworking family, and has chosen to handle all the hoopla of becoming a member of the royal family with grace and ease.

She'll be able to make a difference like Princess Di did by bringing her likeable and powerful celebrity status to make a difference in the lives of people who need help.

So, Kate—Princess Catherine—way to go! Keep modeling fabulousness!

You don't have to be a real-life princess to feel like one. Choose to feel like a princess. Choose to be comfortable in your own skin. Choose to accept compliments and be kind and gracious. Choose to feel fabulous now!

— 16 —

Drawing and Holding Your Boundaries

To feel fabulous, you have to draw boundaries and stick to them. Learning to say no and being firm requires that you first understand why you *don't* say no, and then you have to practice standing up to people who push your boundaries.

"Well, I *meant* to say no." Does this sound familiar? We've all had the experience of saying yes to someone when we intended to say no. We knew it was going to be difficult, but we were determined this time. Then, the next thing we knew, we were saying yes. How did that happen?! *Why* did that happen?

Have you noticed that the very people to whom you mean to say no are the same ones who seem to draw the life energy out of you, and as a result, you cave in to their wishes?

Some people are trained to get their way. They are persistent and determined to get you to say yes to them. And whether they're trained professionally or have just become this way through years of experience, they are highly skilled at getting their wishes met.

At my local car wash, the man who writes up the job ticket is a master at getting people to buy the full works. You know what I'm talking about: the thirty-five-dollar hand wash, hand wax, and air-freshener treatment. I actually can't stand going there because I know each time I'll have to be really strong and almost harsh to get him to back down. Most of the time, I just want a regular wash and wax. "Why would you want the two-dollar wax when, for just a few dollars more, you can upgrade to the eight-dollar treatment?" *Please, just put the wax on the car and let me out of here!*

These people are what I call energy suckers, and you're the energy lollipop. What actually goes on? Let's take a look. . . .

How Do People Get Your Energy?

From a young age, people learn how to control other people to get their way. Here are some of the techniques they use:

- Manipulation
- Acting aloof by pulling away in an attempt to have you chase them
- Money or gifts
- Bullying techniques—verbal, emotional, or physical
- Hostility
- Persistence
- Crying or drama of some sort
- Acting intellectually superior

How Do They Control You?

Whatever they do to control you, there's only one reason why it happens: you allow it. The reason you allow it is because you believe you need something from that particular person. These things can be as important as love, validation, acceptance, approval, a job, or a home, or even something as simple as getting your car washed. Or you allow it because you don't want to be perceived as harsh, uncooperative, unkind, or not nice!

Remember, as I mentioned in another chapter, as women we were raised to be "good" girls—sweet and helpful, not assertive or competitive, and to not create conflict—at any cost.

How to Be Released From Their Control

Whatever your reason is for not maintaining your boundaries with certain people, it will always have the same result: you did not honor yourself. So, the next time you want to say no, look to see what you think you need that might keep you from being firm. Is it love, validation, your job, or a simple need? Once you understand the need, instead of trying to get it from an outside source, give yourself the love, validation, or acceptance. Or let go of needing to be seen a certain way. For instance, I'm willing to be seen as harsh by the car-wash guy.

When you give yourself what you need, you take your energy and power back. Then you will release yourself from the control of others. You'll watch them maneuver to get their way, but you won't succumb to them.

When you connect to an all-loving Divine Source, you

will be filled with love, light, and joy. You will be connected to *the* energy source of the universe. Everything you need and want comes from there.

As long as you continue to think that your mother, father, brother, sister, boyfriend, boss, teacher, spouse, or anyone else is *the* source, you can be controlled. If you remember that you receive everything you need and want when you stay connected to the Divine Source, then you can freely have what you want. There is no cost.

Say yes to Divine Source and no to human control. Say yes to your choices and no to the choices of others that don't serve you. You'll be training people how to treat you. You'll be taking care of yourself.

Handling Backlash From Drawing Boundaries

So now that you understand the importance of sticking to your boundaries, let me share some information that might help you handle the backlash (the disapproval, anger, tears, and so on) you will inevitably receive from drawing them. Handling the backlash is so crucial to the success of drawing and maintaining boundaries that I spend a good bit of time on this subject with my clients. Being kind but firm can help reduce your chances of backlash from some people, but you're still likely to get it from others.

If you've always been the "nice" girl who puts other people's needs first, instead of taking care of yourself first, you've in essence created an unspoken agreement that says their needs come first and your needs come second. So, when you all of a sudden draw a boundary, there will be some uncomfortable repercussions. For instance, if you tell your boss you can't work late tonight, he or she might become angry or aloof; or if you tell your boyfriend you're going out with your girlfriends on Thursday night, he might sulk or go out the next night with his friends and not tell you; or if you tell your friend you don't want to hear her criticisms of your boyfriend anymore, she might get huffy or withdraw and not answer your calls.

Why do they respond this way? It is because you're actually breaking a perceived agreement with that person that says you come second to their wishes, desires, and wants. People get upset when you put them second, especially if they've always been first. They'll probably attempt to manipulate you back into the original agreement so you will cater to their needs first.

This isn't necessarily malicious on their part. They aren't bad people because they're trying to manipulate you into caving in to them. They just liked getting their way, and it was easy before. So they will attempt to restore the "old order." But the methods they use to restore it might not feel good to you. Picture a child in a store throwing a temper tantrum when his mother says he can't have a toy he wants. If the temper tantrum has worked in the past, he'll keep using it because it works. If it hasn't worked, a child will move on to the next tactic. It's normal and healthy for a child to express that he or she is upset, and it is up to the parent to set boundaries to teach the child what is or isn't acceptable. However, some adults, who should know better, might use tactics that aren't so healthy or endearing to watch or experience. People who are used to getting their way and then suddenly don't can be mean, angry, hostile, condescending, weepy, and clingy, and they may try all sorts of other unappealing behavior to get their way as well.

Here are some tips for riding out their tactics until they realize their efforts are futile and finally accept your new boundaries and your new way of being in the relationship: as an equal, which means you will balance your needs with their needs.

Tips for Handling Backlash

- First, expect them to try something to restore the old order.

- Don't take their reactions personally!

- Don't expect people to all of a sudden be delighted that you're taking care of yourself.

- Do give them some time to adjust to the new order that you are now equally important and you are going to take care of yourself.

- Good people will honor your boundaries. Be patient with them and yourself as you're shifting the "agreement."

- When you've had enough of their boundary pushing, tell them so in a kind and firm manner.

I would love to be able to tell you that people will be thrilled that you want to take care of yourself. Sometimes they will be happy for you, but more often than not they will have some reaction. Simply be prepared for backlash, but be careful not to focus on it so much that you end up creating, through the law of attraction, any reactions from people. Again, just be aware of the likelihood.

A little backlash is fine, but don't put up with too much! Stand your ground and maintain your boundary. If someone should become mean or even abusive with their language or attitude, walk away from that person. A healthy human being has a little reaction; an unhealthy human being has a big and prolonged reaction. (I'm assuming you have generally healthy people in your life and you are simply retraining them and yourself to respect your boundaries.)

Here's what you could say to various people when you want the backlash to stop.

In a personal relationship you can say something like this: "You need to get used to me taking care of myself. I'm equally important in this relationship. I hope you'll honor that. It's important for the health of our spirits and our relationship. I love you, and I want what's best for both of us."

In a business relationship, you can tell the boss something along these lines: "I need to leave now so I can be sharp and energetic for work tomorrow." Don't give excuses or rationalizations. Less is more in this scenario. Smile and be firm. You are retraining your boss.

With a friend who always wants to go to the same loud, unhealthy restaurant, tell her no next time she wants you to go there with her. Suggest another restaurant you'd like to try and see what unfolds. Don't put up with any manipulation or excuses she might come up with. If she's really your friend, she'll get it and respect you for standing up for yourself. She'll even willingly go with you to the restaurant of your choice.

Whatever you do, don't cross your boundary by giving in. If you do, you're in essence telling them that you'll talk the talk, but you won't walk the walk. You'll talk about boundaries, but you won't honor them, so they don't have to either.

Drawing boundaries and dealing with the backlash can be difficult. I know. But the rewards are worth every uncomfortable moment. Good people want you to take care of yourself. Like the famous poet Robert Frost said, "Good fences make good neighbors." Well, good boundaries make good friends (or boyfriends, husbands, bosses, and so on).

Honoring yourself by drawing boundaries and standing up for what's important to you is a crucial way for your relationships to flourish and for you to feel fabulous and be filled with love, joy, and respect.

Learn to draw boundaries for the sake of your health, happiness, and self-trust. Be willing to practice saying no and give others a little time to get used to your newfound power. Stick to your boundaries, and you'll feel fabulous!

The Secret to Looking and Feeling Feminine

What determines how feminine you look? Is it your body type? Is it how you dress? Is it your age? Is it whether or not you wear makeup and high heels?

It's none of the above. The answer has to do with the internal, not the external.

The secret to looking and feeling feminine is choosing to be happy. Happiness softens the edges we might have. It gives us a sense of ease and flow. And that is truly what makes a woman feel and therefore be feminine.

Think about how you feel when you're happy. Usually you're smiling, your energy is lighter, and your heart is more open. You can light up a room with your good energy. And when you're happy, you're more likely to wear clothes that either make you feel comfortable and relaxed, and/or are incredibly flattering.

Can clothing enhance that feeling? Sure. Does your body

type reflect that feeling? No. What reflects femininity is how you move in the world. And how you move in the world comes from how you feel about yourself and your life. And if you don't feel happy right this minute, realize you can choose to think a happy thought and, in a moment, change to being and reflecting happiness.

One of the actual definitions of feminine is: *Possessing qualities or characteristics considered typical of or appropriate to a woman.* So that means if you're a woman, then you're feminine.

So how come at times we don't feel feminine? When I was in Hawaii, I spent some time thinking about this subject and watching women move around the Big Island. One thing I noticed is that women who were relaxed looked more feminine. Women who were stressed and controlling seemed less feminine.

So is stress one of the factors that, at times, makes you feel less feminine? I think so. Have you ever seen a really beautifully put-together woman with a scowl on her face? Is she appealing? No. Do you think of her as feminine? No. Usually you don't want to be around her—and that goes for men and women.

Another factor that can make you feel less feminine is adopting a tough facade to feel safe and protective of your body and heart. Sometimes you don't want to come off as feminine, and that's an acceptable choice. Just be aware that you're making that choice, and make it consciously and appropriately but not continually. If you find yourself continuing to put up a tough facade, please get some help with boundaries and developing trust so that you can feel safe again.

Remember, once you put up a protective barrier, you won't feel feminine. And that's fine. You don't need to feel feminine all the time. It's when you never feel feminine or you think it comes from the external that it causes you to feel inadequate compared to other women. That's an awful feeling, and it's not true. You're never inadequate compared to anyone. All women have challenges they are dealing with or will deal with at some point in their lives.

What Can You Do to Feel Feminine?

We associate softness and gentleness with femininity. It's easy to be soft and gentle when you're relaxed at the beach, sitting at home reading a good book, or laughing with friends. It's easy to be soft and gentle when you're feeling safe and relaxed.

So do something relaxing. Get a massage. Go on vacation. Get some exercise and burn off the tension. Have a cocktail with a friend in a beautiful setting. Take a yoga class and stretch your body. Take the weekend off, and curl up and read a book. Get back in touch with yourself without the stress.

Once you get relaxed again, you'll feel softer, gentler, and feminine again. And then you'll move around the world reflecting that femininity. If it is your intention, you will attract men when you are more relaxed and happy since those are qualities that attract them. A good man wants to be around a woman who takes care of herself, sees the world through a positive filter, finds the good in life, has fun, and chooses to be happy.

More important than how a man thinks about you is that

you like yourself better when you take care of yourself, see your life as a series of positive experiences, and choose to be happy and have fun.

Starting now, if you want to look and feel feminine, work from the inside out, and you will feel good in a matter of minutes. The great spiritual teachers tell us to focus on a positive thought for sixty-seven seconds. That's all it takes to change your thoughts. Feeling feminine is just a perk, a by-product of being happy. Get a little dress, a pair of shorts and a fun T-shirt, or a pretty blouse and great-fitting skirt. Wear your new outfit with fun, colorful sandals. Paint your toenails a bright color, like electric blue or pearly coral. Anything, just have fun. Play! You can choose to be happy and playful!

As a woman, feeling feminine is a choice we can make anytime. Choose to allow yourself to feel feminine by relaxing, being gentle and soft with yourself, wearing something pretty, and being happy with your life.

—◈ 18 ◈—
Seeing the Light...
in Your Self

One of the greatest gifts we give to ourselves is to *see* ourselves. One of the greatest gifts we give to others is to *see* them.

I love coaching because it's a perfect venue for allowing me to truly see other people. What a joy it is to spend my days *seeing* great women and men—seeing them for who they truly are. Imagine the gift to my soul of being permitted to teach precious souls to see themselves and then to let others see them as well.

It is when you want others to see you without seeing yourself that you hit a snag. Have you ever snagged your sweater on something? If so, you know that it is relatively easy to unsnag it. You also get snagged when you want someone to see you, but you won't show yourself. That's a setup. Be careful here; the ego will try to convince you that someone has to see you before you can reveal yourself. It doesn't work that way.

You're wanting and waiting for someone to validate you.
But it's not going to happen. Why not?

Well, others can only see what we show them, and they can only see what they are capable of seeing.

After almost thirty years of working on myself, I can now see great depth, wisdom, love, compassion, kindness, sadness, sorrow, joy, pain, creativity, excitement, and passion in others, because I see and experience them in myself. If I were a person who didn't go to great depth in myself, I would be unable to see depth in others. If I weren't creative, then I wouldn't recognize and certainly couldn't validate someone else's creativity.

I wasn't always comfortable with anger, so I used to shy away from a client who was angry. However, now that I've let myself experience anger—there's so much energy in anger— I'm not afraid to *see* it and let a client share it. In the past, though, because I was uncomfortable with anger, I might have tried to talk my client out of being angry. These days, I've been known to provoke anger to give clients something to push against.

It's no one's fault that they can't validate or *see* you; either they have those qualities or they don't. Sometimes people reject certain qualities in themselves and then really don't want to acknowledge them in you. They cannot—not until they embrace that quality in themselves. Often, when we're still young, we don't yet have the experience or the depth to *see* things in other people. Too often, a woman who feels "rejected," may go into hiding or wait for a man to validate her. Even if someone comes along to validate her, she is not likely to believe his assurances about how wonderful she is if she doesn't already believe it about herself.

Do You Want to *See* Yourself?

I know you know that there are special things about you—even if you can only remember glimpses of them from your childhood. Those qualities are still there. In *The Four Agreements,* don Miguel Ruiz talks about how as children we become "domesticated" by our parents. We learn to behave in a way that makes Mommy and Daddy happy, and then they give us love. The trouble with doing so is that we aren't being ourselves so we lose sight of who we are. We lose sight of what makes us special and unique. As a coach, I encourage my clients to explore what makes them special and guide them to get back in touch with their uniqueness. And this way, my clients are once again able to see themselves.

So before you set yourself up again to get someone to validate you, I want you to realize that other people can't do that. It's impossible. Don't even try. It's a recipe for disaster. Validate yourself. Only you have the power to do that. Then once you're in touch with what's precious about your self, let others see it.

Something to *See* About Men

Generally speaking, men aren't mind readers, but women often want men to *see* them without making too much effort to be seen. They want men to do all of the pursuing and all the asking. Men are supposed to know what a woman wants, where she wants to go, and when and how she wants to be asked out.

It's important to know that men are insecure too. You should hear them from my perspective. *Should I pay? Should I open the door? What should I wear?* Most men aren't comfortable in the relationship arena, but they are trying. Please cut them some slack. They'll work hard, but don't make it impossible for them. Don't set them up. Show them what is precious about you. *See* what is precious about them. They will love you for it—if they're developed and stable.

Let me give you an example. I've been married twenty-two years. The other day, I realized something about my husband and decided to share it with him in a card. On the outside of the envelope, I wrote, "Mighty Soul." In twenty-two years, I have never seen his face light up the way it did when he read that. You'd have thought I just handed him a pot of gold. Evidently, what I gave him was even better than gold. It was the gift of *seeing* him. He *is* a mighty soul. It fits him perfectly.

If you like to light other people up, look to see what you see in them and tell them. If you want to light yourself up, look to see what is magnificent about you and tell your self. Then go out in the world and be that mighty soul, that uplifting source of energy, that gentle spirit, that kind heart, or that soft place to land. Whatever it is: Be it. Live it. Share it.

Someone special will ultimately *see* you. They will recognize your qualities. They will want to be part of your life. In the meantime, you'll be enjoying life, not hiding from it.

Choose to see yourself. Ask others (friends, coworkers, family, even exes) what they *see* in you. They'll tell you. And if they can't, it's not because you don't have anything special, it's because they can't see it in themselves. Turn around and share something that you see and value in them.

Show your precious self. Don't wait for others to see and validate you. You are a precious child of Divine Source. Come out, come out, wherever you are! I see and honor you. Choose to see yourself. Choose to see others. Choose to let others see you.

— 19 —
Stop and Listen to Your Wise Voice!

I recently spent a lovely week in Nantucket, Massachusetts, with my husband's side of the family. We had a lot of fun talking, eating, playing with babies, shopping, and exercising.

I was out walking one morning and watched a bicyclist go through a stop sign and run right into a car. She flew over the car and fortunately landed on the grass. Since she was wearing a helmet, her head was fine, but her ankle was badly broken. I stayed with her until the ambulance arrived, helping her stay calm and taking as much of her pain as I could and replacing it with love.

Afterward, I stopped to say a prayer for the speedy and proper healing of her ankle, and I started thinking about the whole concept of "not stopping."

What I realized is that "not stopping" comes from our ego telling us that "stopping" is something negative. For each person, it's different. I can hear the ego say things like, "If I stop,

I'll lose time," or "I can't stop; I have to keep working on this to get it perfect," or "If I stop, I won't be as successful as I want to be."

At the root of all our excuses for not stopping is a negative thought about ourselves. It is driven by how we think others will perceive us and/or how we perceive ourselves. The ego (that gremlin!) loves to tell you that stopping means something negative about you, when, actually, the opposite is true.

Let's look at where you might need to stop. Are you working too hard and not taking time to exercise? Are you charging money on your credit cards instead of creating the money through the law of attraction? Are you letting your negative self-talk drain your energy? Are you putting off talking to your partner/friend/boss about something that is bothering you?

Are you working on the to-do list and not taking time for self-care? You know it's never going to get completed because it's always going to be replenished. When you take time to take care of your self, you will have more energy to complete your list—not that you want completion to be your goal. It can be a good rationalization if you want one. So instead of saying, "I don't have time to take a hot bath" or "I don't have time to just sit for fifteen minutes and read my favorite magazine," try giving yourself permission and notice what happens when you do.

Most important, whatever you are doing that isn't working . . . STOP! Take a moment to rethink your decision to *not* stop. Don't let your ego—that voice in your head that often drives you to do things that are ultimately harmful—run the show. Listen to your inner wisdom. You have a wise voice.

You came here to have a joyful life and to create. You are more joyful and creative when you are relaxed, eat well, exercise regularly, don't get yourself into debt, and talk and act lovingly to yourself. Stop the ego and let your loving wise voice take the lead. It will always guide you in the right direction.

Spicy, Saucy, and Hot!

I had one of the most amazing, soul-transporting experiences of my life not long ago. It's the kind of experience that reminds me of how truly glorious life is when I open myself to receiving the gifts of my fellow humans. It also reminded me that being spicy, saucy, and hot is a feeling. It's an attitude. And it's fun!

My husband and I went to the San Diego Jazz Party and spent three days listening to sixteen amazingly gifted musicians who are at the top of their field. They range in age from their early thirties to their late eighties. These aren't simply good musicians; these are *great* musicians.

All weekend long they played and jammed from the depths of their hearts and souls so that we could experience their gifts. I can only imagine what it must have felt like for them to give their gift so freely and deeply.

Then on Saturday night, the experience went from amazing

to mind-blowing. The headliner for the party was Jeannie Cheatham. Jeannie sings and plays piano. She rocks my soul with her soulful, powerful voice; lively piano playing; earthy, bluesy style; inexhaustible energy; and sassy attitude. Jeannie's specialty is the Kansas City blues. While many of the musicians were jazz specialists, they easily transitioned to the blues to keep up with her.

I was on my feet cheering, clapping, and dancing during her brilliant performances. Jeannie's energy and power is a gift from Divine Source, enhanced by her lifetime desire and discipline to follow her dream and not let a mountain of obstacles stop her.

Jeannie's husband, Jimmy Cheatham—a gifted bass trombonist—had just transitioned that past January. I had wondered if Jeannie would feel up to performing. Well, not only was she up to it, it seemed to be exactly what she needed.

Jeannie is spicy, saucy, and hot!

During her set on Sunday, an older woman, clearly miffed about something, walked up to me and told me she was leaving early because she couldn't stand Jeannie. I was surprised, but smiled slightly to acknowledge her departure and turned my attention back to the performance. Later that evening during the car ride home, I mentioned to my husband what the woman had said. We discussed it and concluded that Jeannie's "sassy mama" vocals and piano were simply too much for that woman.

Jeannie had turned seventy-nine years old that year and was still performing with as much energy, if not more, than a younger woman. The lady who claimed to me that she "couldn't stand Jeannie" was about that same age. I couldn't imagine being turned off by such a spicy, saucy, hot, mind-blowingly gifted musician playing her heart out in a bright red dress (for good luck and good energy).

So what's my point?

No matter what age you are, you need to allow yourself the experience of being spicy, saucy, and hot from time to time. If you don't, you might end up resenting (or not being able "to stand") another woman who is, regardless of your age or hers.

I sure felt spicy, saucy, and hot listening to that music, from the first number to the last. Jazz and blues makes me want to move, sing, feel, and live. So for me, music is one key to feeling spicy, saucy, and hot.

Jeannie is my model for how I want to be now and how I want to be when I'm pushing eighty.

A Goddess in Action

During the performance, Jeannie did something that moved me to tears. As if she wasn't already showing me and other open-minded women our own potential for living and feeling fabulous, she took things a step further. When I realized the power of what she was doing, I knew I was witnessing a Goddess in action. She called forth each of the musicians to give more of themselves, not for her sake, for theirs. After each musician appeared to be finishing their solo, she would say, "Eddie, give me a little more of that guitar," and Eddie would give her more. Then she would call out for him to give her even more, and he would. On and on, it went like that with each musician—tenor sax, the bass, trombone, and drums.

They let it rip. She called them forth, urging them to give more and more of themselves and their gifts.

You could see the musicians' sheer delight when they were in the middle of it. And, when they finished, even they were blown away by how deeply they reached and what they gave. It wasn't about her—it was about her sharing the stage and calling on the other members of the band to feel and share their gifts.

What Are the Powerful Gifts Here for You?

Look to see where you are holding yourself back. Where do you want to let it rip? Then set up an action plan to do one thing this month. And do it!

Where or what would you like to see more of from others in your life—for their sake, not yours? Call them forth; they will love you for it.

And what do you want to do to feel spicy, saucy, and hot? It's not about how you look. Jeannie was seventy-nine. If she could be that way, so can you. It's a feeling. It's not about how thin or curvy you are. It's not about the shape of your nose, legs, or waist. It's not about your age. It's not external. It's a feeling. It's an attitude. It's a choice!

I know you don't want to choose to be the old woman who left in a huff because she was threatened by another woman's pulsating sauciness. I know that deep in your soul you want to be—even if just for a day—a spicy, saucy, hot woman who gives it her all.

Maybe you want to buy and wear a fun red dress. Maybe you want to put on some sassy music and dance around the house. Maybe you want to take your boyfriend, husband, or friend to a club to hear some jazz and blues. I encourage you to wear your red dress and feel the music in your body and your soul.

You can choose to be spicy. You can choose to be saucy. You can choose to be hot. You can choose when, where, and with whom. You can choose to give it your all. You can choose to call others forth for their sakes. You can choose to be a Goddess!

—⌐ 21 ⌐—

Assume the Positive!

If you're like many people, you feel unhappy, angry, or hurt when something that you didn't want to happen happens. If so, you're probably having those reactions because you assumed the negative instead of the positive.

Let me give you an example of a negative assumption and a possible undesirable outcome from it. Suppose a new guy you've been dating for a few months doesn't call you for five days. Then when he calls you, you're cold because you think he isn't all that interested in you. After all, you negatively assume, if he was really interested he wouldn't have let five days go by without calling. That would be assuming the negative! Your negative energy that was a result of your negative assumption could turn him off or confuse him and he might never call again.

How would it look if you assumed the positive? The truth is you don't know why he didn't call for five days. Maybe he really was busy with a big project and wanted to talk to you when he wasn't so stressed. Maybe he thought he shouldn't appear too eager. Or maybe he has a full life. All those reasons would make him a healthy man—a good guy to keep moving forward with. If you assumed the positive, you'd be open and light and you'd eventually ask, if he hadn't already told you, what he's been up to or what had been going on in his life. (It's my experience that men will tell you things if they don't feel pressured.) Then, you would be able to determine what had really been going on during his five-day absence. If it was fine with you—he'd been working on a huge project or he thought he should not be persistent—then you would exude a positive vibe and he would get your positive energy and likely call again.

Let's look at another example. Suppose a girlfriend didn't want to go somewhere with you. Maybe you wanted to go to dinner after work, and she didn't want to go. Under the negative assumption, you would assume she didn't want to spend time with you. Under the positive assumption, you would assume she wanted to take care of herself and you would support her in that choice. That's what so great about friends—we usually don't bring negative assumptions into the relationship.

Another example might revolve around the treatment you got from a doctor, coworker, or boss. People can be cross and cranky at times. If you make a negative assumption, you'll think they did it intentionally or that they don't like you. If you make a positive assumption, you'll ask, when they calm down, if they're okay. Or you'll wait for a more appropriate time and tell them you wish to be treated differently.

Assuming the positive goes for partners not doing things, friends not calling, or people being late. Every circumstance and every communication falls under this concept.

When you start with the positive assumption, your life will be completely different. You won't get angry, hurt, or annoyed. I'm not saying to not communicate with others when something doesn't work for you—for instance, if a friend is consistently late or your husband is always forgetting to take out the trash. I'm referring to the isolated incidents that occur in your interactions with friends, family, and coworkers. They will more likely be isolated incidents rather than regular occurrences if you assume positive intentions. From the place of positive intentions, you'll be more compassionate, open, curious, and helpful. You'll be more successful and have more fun. You'll spend less time in the negative and more time in the positive, which is always better for your heart and soul. You'll communicate clearly and without drama.

It's a CHOICE! You can assume the negative or you can assume the positive! Try the positive. Practice making positive assumptions for one full week. You'll be amazed at how often you used to assume the negative in the past.

When you switch to assuming the positive, you will love the results. You will attract all sorts of opportunities, love, and great times. You'll feel fabulous and free! It's a choice. Assume the positive!

22

"Be the Hope"

After Hurricane Katrina, many artists gave performances to raise money for the victims. I was fortunate to be able to attend a benefit performance for the victims of the disaster that featured some amazing artists, including k.d. lang and Jackson Browne. It was held at a local church in my town, and the theme of the benefit was "Be the Hope."

The minister of the church opened the benefit by sharing her belief that we need to "be the hope." There were four families at the performance that had lost everything in the hurricane, but they did not lose the most important thing. They chose to hold on to the one thing that wind, water, and others could never take from them: HOPE.

How often do we lose hope? How often does our ego toss things at us that seem to force the hope right out of our hearts and souls?

Someone breaks up with you and you lose hope that you

will ever have love again. You lose your job and lose hope that you will ever find a good-paying job again. Or you find out you have a disease, and you lose hope that you will be healthy again.

The gremlin can really torment you. It can tell you things like, "See, I told you no one would ever love you," or "I knew you couldn't get pregnant," or "I told you the job was too much for you," or "You know you'll never be healthy again. Feel fabulous? Who are you kidding?"

I want you to take back your power from the ego and know that there is energy in the Universe that is the source of love, healing, renewal. (Throughout this book, I've been referring to this energy as Divine Source.) Knowing that energy exists and that it loves and provides for you brings hope.

Most of us haven't lost everything, but it can feel like it at times, and the gremlin convinces us we should give up hope. Yet there were four families without money, cars, jobs, homes, or clothes who hadn't given up. And as a result, people who cared and were willing to be the hope, to be the light to guide them back to joy and prosperity, surrounded them.

Consciously choosing hope is what's required to change how you feel and what you'll receive. Why? Because without hope, you'll usually feel pessimistic or negative. If you feel pessimistic, you feel you won't receive what you need or want. And if you don't feel open to receiving, you'll miss opportunities: you won't ask people for help, you won't go to the networking meeting that day, you won't return a phone call from a prospective client, or you won't look at your e-mails to see if you've heard from someone. You'll block the Universe with your negativity. You'll block Divine Source. Remember, we have free will so we can choose either hope or pessimism.

The Law of Attraction teaches us that we get what we think about whether we want it or not. So if you're thinking positively and hopefully, you'll attract good things into your life. If you're thinking negatively or pessimistically, you'll attract not-so-good things into your life. Or you just won't attract anything you've been asking for and wanting to receive.

Hope is a choice made from your heart and soul. Loss of hope—pessimism—is a choice made from your gremlin. It's all about fear. I'll never have (*fill in the blank*) again. Yes, choosing hope is the more challenging choice. But it's also the more rewarding and uplifting choice. And from the place of hope, you *can* receive.

So, if you're finding yourself in a situation where you have lost hope, reach out and ask someone for help. Say a prayer and just know that it will be answered. When you choose hope, you are creating a positive energy field around you that draws positive and helpful people and situations to you.

Most important of all—BE THE HOPE— for someone less fortunate than you. That will serve to remind you of all you have. And there is no better way to feel fabulous than to give to others and be the light for them during their dark time. Choose hope for yourself and others.

23

Believe Your Way to Winning!

One day Elizabeth, a former client, called me to celebrate a huge win in her life. She had just closed a gigantic consulting deal and was overflowing with joy and excitement. I was genuinely thrilled for her, and then she said, "It's all thanks to you."

Here's something I want you to know about me: I'm not going to let a client give me the credit for their victory. I will share in the joy of their accomplishment, but the client gets the credit since it's the client who does the work. I just believe in them until they believe in themselves.

Believing in herself was what it took for Elizabeth to succeed. She knew instantly that she and her team were perfect for the job. She got the job because she believed in herself, her team, and the work they could do.

I want to share with you why this is so important and is not just another victory. Elizabeth had a lot of responsibilities.

She was a single mom of three teenagers and was the legal guardian of her late sister's two teenagers.

Her marriage ended and her business collapsed, and Elizabeth found herself with five teenagers to feed and no one to rely on but herself. Through coaching with me, she realized she wasn't alone. Divine Source was with her every step of the way. She quit her job, which could no longer support her and the children due to unfair restructuring of her commission, and bravely started her own company. Starting a new business requires a huge leap of faith. And as always, when we believe, when we have hope, Divine Source can help us. Elizabeth received this help, but she did the work and she stayed hopeful. She believed in her abilities, and she trusted Divine Source.

Here's the interesting thing about how this unfolded: The offer letter for the consulting deal had landed in her e-mail junk mail, which she didn't check on a regular basis. (Remember, five teenagers, single-mom scenario.) The offer was due to expire, but Elizabeth listened to an inner voice that told her to check her junk mail. And there was this gigantic offer letter!

Believe in yourself. Believe that Divine Source will help you if you show up and do the work and trust.

My Other Favorite Women Winners

J.K. Rowling went from being unemployed to becoming the hugely successful author of the Harry Potter series of books. Evidently, her first book had been rejected by twelve publishers before she found one to accept her book. (Smart publisher!) It is a good thing she didn't stop believing in herself.

In 1963, Mary Kay Ash quit her job after being passed over for promotion. With a $5,000 investment, she started Mary Kay Cosmetics. Her philosophy is: "If you think you can, you can. If you think you can't, you're right." This is right along the lines of "Be the Hope" (see page 113). In 2008, Mary Kay Cosmetics had 1.7 million consultants and sales in excess of 2.2 billion dollars. Thank goodness for her that she got passed over for a promotion!

And the all-important success story to women—Oprah Winfrey. I almost don't have to say anything because virtually every one of us knows her story and that her level of success is off the charts. She's the first African-American woman to become a billionaire. What I love is that she turned down a job offer early in her career that would have stuck her in a too small city and limited her visibility. Her "father" wanted her to go for the security of the job, but she chose not to go for security and instead to believe in herself. Thank you, Oprah, for being willing to model believing your way to winning!

Each of these women has her strengths and weaknesses. We have strengths and weaknesses too. We accomplish things in life by focusing on our strengths.

Believe in Your Strengths

What are your strengths? What are your gifts? What do you do well? You know. Don't let your ego talk you out of them. Often your strengths and gifts are the very things you take for granted. So if you hear your mind dismiss something, stop and write it down. I guarantee it will be a strength.

I'll give you an example: when I'm coaching, I can quickly

see what's blocking someone from moving forward in their life. I never talked about it because I just figured all coaches had the same experience. I hear certain keywords more distinctly than other things the client is saying. I even see words or phrases a client says in neon lights. I don't have to struggle; it just comes.

Now, wouldn't you think I'd share that with potential new clients? For nine years, I never said a word. I just took it for granted. But it's a strength and a gift. And now I share it so that I can help people make an informed decision about whether or not they want to coach with me. If I don't tell them, how will they know what I bring to the coaching process? The difference is talking about our strengths from our heart, not from our ego. From the ego, it sounds like bragging and can feel like bragging; from the heart, it's a warm, wonderful fact.

Are you are a fast thinker, witty, friendly, funny, kind, compassionate, creative, thoughtful, sincere, responsible, loving, warm, intelligent, giving, generous, a problem solver, a team player, a good number-two person, a leader, an implementer, a great cupcake baker, a wonderful hostess, or skilled in photography, drawing, painting?

Name your strengths. Focus on those. Once you have them listed, think about how those strengths have served you. Maybe they served you in your family—did you keep the peace or come up with the ideas for fun outings? Maybe they served you at work—are you always organizing and helping people simplify their work? Maybe they served you in relationships—are you the loving and nurturing one, the one who cooks and loves entertaining?

The key is to embrace your strengths and be clear about who you are. Know who you are in your heart. You don't need to be someone else to attract a spouse, a job, friends, or anything. You get to be yourself and thoroughly enjoy that. It's so much easier, fun, and rewarding!

Here are three affirmations I want you to say a few times every day. Get relaxed before you repeat them. You need to be in a place of feeling good about yourself before affirmations work. So take a bath, read a magazine, go for a walk, watch the sunset, and then settle into a comfy chair or your bed, then repeat:

"I believe in myself !" "I love and accept myself as a precious and beautiful woman." "I feel fabulous today and every day."

You can replace these or combine them with any other affirmations that resonate with you. Do them faithfully for twenty-one days—the time it takes to make a change—and see how you feel.

Honestly, if you thought you could feel better about yourself and live the life you desire, wouldn't you make time daily for three affirmations? You bet. Well try it. What have you got to lose, except your tormenting ego?!

Believe in your gifts and strengths. They were given to you so you could thrive in this lifetime. Choose to develop them and let them flourish. Believe in yourself, and you will feel fabulous forever!

—⚬ 24 ⚬—
What's Determination Got to Do With It? Everything!

What's the one thing you are determined to do differently in your life starting right now? With a healthy dose of determination, you can accomplish it. *The American Heritage Dictionary* definition of determination is "firmness of purpose, resolve." We see it every day in young and old alike.

Children and Determination

I've always enjoyed this quote by poet Myra Cohn Livingston:

> Hey, this little kid gets roller skates. She puts them on. She stands up and almost flops over backward. She sticks out a foot like she's going somewhere and falls down and smacks her hand. She grabs hold of a step to get up and sticks out the other foot and slides about six inches and falls and skins her knee. And then, you know what? She brushes off the dirt and blood and puts some spit on it and then sticks out the other foot again.

I've noticed that determination is a powerful motivator. Do you remember learning to skate or ride a bike or play a musical instrument? Have you watched a toddler learn to walk? Talk about determination. They're loaded with it. They fall, clap their hands, get back up, and try again. They fall, laugh, and try again—probably about a hundred times before they master it. Think about it: you didn't give up trying to learn to walk. Small children don't have egos that tell them they probably can't succeed so they should just stick to crawling for the rest of their lives.

Girls and Determination

One of the most powerful examples of determination in a teenager is Bethany Hamilton, the surfer who lost her left arm in a shark attack in 2003. She not only learned to surf again but also went on to win first place in the NSSA National Championship, a goal she had been trying to achieve since the accident.

If you're not familiar with surfing, getting out beyond the waves is the hardest part for most surfers and you usually need both your arms to accomplish that task. Surfing requires endurance, a strong core, and tremendous upper-body strength. Bethany was at a huge disadvantage to surf, much less to surf competitively. But she didn't give up. Her courage and determination won out over her fear, her frustration, and her trauma. I don't know about you, but I figure if Bethany can surf again and win surfing contests against the best women competitive surfers, the rest of us can do anything we set our hearts and minds to accomplish as well. The 2011 movie *Soul*

Surfer based on Bethany's experience can be an inspiration to us all, whether or not we want to surf.

Women and Determination

One of my favorite examples of a determined woman is Immaculée Ilibagiza, who was determined to survive the Rwandan genocide. In 1994, she and seven other women hid in a local pastor's bathroom that was 3 feet long by 4 feet wide for ninety-one days while machete-wielding killers hunted for them. Her mother, father, and two brothers were killed during the genocide, and nearly a million people were also killed during the three-month reign of terror. And as if surviving wasn't enough, what is truly amazing about her is the forgiveness she was able to find in her heart. She actually sought out the killers of her family and forgave them. Her book, *Left to Tell: Discovering God Amidst the Rwandan Holocaust,* which has sold 250,000 copies, is a beautiful story of her journey and her discovery of the power of prayer, unconditional love, and her deep faith in God. Dr. Wayne Dyer considers her to be a "uniquely Divine woman." Others have recognized her efforts to help those left behind in Rwanda. In 2007, Immaculée was the recipient of the Mahatma Gandhi Reconciliation and Peace Award, an award given to those who inspire young people to make a commitment to non-violence, forgiveness, and reconciliation.

What Are You Determined to Do?

When I ask you what you are determined to do, I'm not

talking about competing or trying to survive in a war-torn country. Each one of us has something we want to do or change or become, something we want to bring into our lives, complete, or change. This isn't about ego; this is about your heart's desire and your willingness to be determined to accomplish your dream.

What are you determined to have or do this year? Start right now to make that happen.

It can be a simple thing, like wanting to wear skirts more often this summer. Or maybe you want to learn to swim, water ski, sail, or Rollerblade. Maybe you want to complete a photo album or change your hairstyle. Maybe you want to read a book you've put aside or take a long overdue vacation. Or it can be something on a larger scale: maybe there is someone you want to forgive, or maybe you'd like to forgive yourself.

Bethany Hamilton endured pain and frustration and found the courage to believe in herself and compete professionally. Immaculée Ilibagiza endured terror and overwhelming odds against her very survival and turned the experience into an opportunity to connect more deeply with God and to feel the freedom of forgiveness.

If you've tried something and it didn't go as well as you wanted it to, DON'T GIVE UP. And if you haven't started but want to, NOW IS THE TIME!

Ego, Relationships, and Determination

The only part of you that gives up is the mind or ego. The heart knows what it wants—it doesn't stop beating or desiring. The soul knows it's all about love. Only the ego challenges you to believe that you're too old, young, skinny, fat, too educated, not educated enough, too successful, not successful enough. Oh, the ego can go on and on and on and on.

Don't listen to it! Be determined. Fill yourself with a firmness of purpose to not let it spoil things anymore and a resolve to silence it.

Be determined to feel fabulous! Be determined to believe in yourself! Be determined to hope again! You weren't meant to crawl. Dust yourself off and start all over again. Determination is a choice. A great choice. Fill yourself with a firmness of purpose and resolve.

25

Living Softly

One winter, my husband and I spent nine glorious days at the beautiful resort Casa del Mar in Baja. Baja is a several-hundred-mile-long sliver of desert bordered by the Sea of Cortez on one side and the Pacific Ocean on the other.

The power and beauty of the ocean always fills me with peaceful energy. The waves can sometimes be so rough that they knock you right off your feet and toss you up into in the air, or so gentle that they allow you to float peacefully on the surface with the warmth of the sun on your face.

One day, we ventured to a beach where the locals swim. The undertow is minimal, so it's safe for children. As I was getting out of the water, I got knocked off my feet and landed on my rump. Tiny stones gathered in my bathing-suit bottom. It was actually funny, and yet, I was reminded of what it feels like to encounter rough energy. It's often sudden, unsettling, and uncomfortable.

Feeling Soft and Graceful

The people in Mexico have always been among my favorite. They are heart-centered people who take care of their spirits and bodies. They take afternoon siestas, work for a few more hours, and then have dinner under the stars in their beautiful, fragrant, flower-filled courtyard gardens. There is an ease with which they live and move.

There is softness in the air in Baja. The women there are soft and sensual. Generally, Mexican women don't believe that they must be skinny to be sexy. They seem to float around with grace, and their warm hearts lift my spirits whenever I encounter them.

When I was young, I didn't feel soft or graceful. In my twenties and thirties, I was a driven businesswoman, trying to prove my worth. I was always comparing myself to other women, and I didn't like myself very much. Things only changed for me after I became gravely ill due to the complications of anorexia. Thereafter, I had a lot of work to do unlearning things that were not good for me and then learning, with help, how to feel soft and sensual.

During this particular trip to Baja, I noticed that a lot of vacationing women didn't like themselves. I could feel and see it in their facial expressions, the way they carried themselves, the way they spoke, and in their energy fields. They were tense, rigid, uptight, and uncomfortable in their skin. I recognized it because I had been there.

Why Women Don't Like Themselves

I began to wonder why so many women don't like themselves. As a coach, I know that it has nothing to do with how a woman looks, how much money she makes, what kind of family she's from, or if she has a boyfriend or husband. I think most women have gotten disconnected from their true selves. They've forgotten how to be fluid, soft, and sensual. They've forgotten what there is to like about being a woman. As a result, women compare themselves to other women to figure out what they are supposed to be. They always find something better in the other women and then put themselves down. Sound familiar? If it does, I want you to promise yourself you'll immediately stop the self-criticism and consider what I'm about to share with you.

Who Are We?

The yogis tell us we aren't our bodies. We are more than our jobs and our roles in life. So if we aren't our bodies, our jobs, or our roles in life, then who are we? We are spiritual beings having a human experience as women, and that, in and of itself, is fabulous!

Think about it. Watch women. We're loving, kind, strong, and beautiful—each warm and friendly in our own way. We love our friends and show it. We compliment each other. We share from our hearts. We laugh with each other in a shared experience. We listen to each other, shop together, cook together, raise children, and nurture our families and friends. What isn't there to like about all of those things?

When did we decide that the shape of our nose, legs, teeth, and other parts of our anatomy had anything to do with whether or not we liked ourselves? I'm not even talking about loving ourselves. This is just *like*.

You are a Goddess! Stop comparing your outer life with anyone else's. If you want something different, find out if you really want it, then go for it.

Choosing to Live Softly

When you choose what feels good, when you are in harmony with your spirit, when you are connected to your heart, when you aren't comparing yourself to others and you are instead living your own truth, you exude peacefulness and softness.

Softness in a woman doesn't have anything to do with her size or culture or race. It's a feminine gentleness that speaks powerfully and truthfully. Some women have asked me how to be soft. I have five steps to help you get there, but first, remember that you *are* soft. Even if you don't feel like it now, you started off that way. Think of a baby girl. She's all softness and love. That's you too.

FIVE STEPS TO SOFTNESS

1 **Relax.** Think about when you feel your softest. It's probably when you're relaxed—for example, after you've had a massage or spent a day at the beach, or had a quiet afternoon at home reading and napping, or engaged in a restorative yoga session or deep meditation. The key is relaxation. Make allowing yourself to relax a priority.

2 **Trust and Be Gentle.** The second step is to be gentle. In order to be gentle, you have to trust yourself and Divine Source. When you trust and feel supported, you can be gentle and peaceful. A woman who trusts Divine Source is easier to be around. She isn't tense or edgy. She's not trying to prove her worth. She isn't competitive. She knows things will work out in her best interest. She's easy, open, and receptive, and flows with whatever is happening.

3 **Be Kind.** Kindness is the third step. Be kind to yourself, your family, your friends, and even strangers. Kindness brings softness with it.

4 **Be Loving.** When you extend love to others, they pick it up, even if they don't realize where it's coming from. And you get the benefits of loving, which is your heart's expression of its true purpose. That also brings you peace, joy, health, abundance, and freedom.

5 **Soothe Yourself.** Do things that soothe your spirit and your heart. This is different from relaxing. It's an actual conscious choice to soothe. Put your hand on your tummy when you're feeling anxious or afraid. Stroke the side of your face the way a mother strokes her baby. Talk soothingly to yourself when you're upset, with a calm, quiet, soothing tone.

If you are relaxed, gentle, kind, loving, soothing, and trusting of Divine Source, do you think you'll like yourself better? You bet! And then will you feel yourself becoming soft? You will! And, when you feel soft, do you like yourself better? Definitely. Will other people want to be around you then? Yes! And most important, you'll enjoy being with yourself!

To feel and live softly once again, know that you live in a loving and supportive Universe. You are loved and supported by a Divine Source. Be gentle, kind, and soothing with yourself and others. Choose this as a way of life. Choose to be the real you—a soft woman.

26

The Complete Secret to Receiving What You Want to Have or Feel!

I want to share with you my thoughts about what I know is necessary in order to receive everything you want to feel and have. I've spent more than thirty years studying many brilliant spiritual teachings on many fascinating subjects. The subject of receiving what you want, need, and desire is always an important one to understand. Many people have written on the subject of manifesting. To me, there's a difference between manifesting and receiving. When I think of manifesting, I feel separate from Divine Source. I feel like I'm the one doing it, and I don't believe that's how this Universe works. So I've replaced the word "manifest" with "receive" because that word makes me feels like I'm connected to Divine Source. It feels like I'm not alone, and that I'm not doing it all by myself. And since I'm not actually doing it all by myself, I feel great accepting that truth.

The following ideas have been the greatest help in my life and in the lives of my clients. Allow me to share them with you now.

What's the real secret to receiving what you want and desire? It starts with the realization that there is a Divine Source in this Universe and that we are an extension of that Divine Source energy in human form. We are that energy having a physical experience. So we are part of Divine Source.

Without the awareness and the understanding that Divine Source is the funnel through which all things come into being—ideas, gifts, love, power, ideas, all of creation—we are left with the erroneous belief that it's just our thoughts and actions, alone, that create.

But in reality, Divine Source is the creator, and as an extension of that energy here on earth, we receive from Divine Source. So wouldn't we want to be aware of that connection? If you want your life to flow easily, effortlessly, and joyfully, you *do* want to be conscious of the connection.

Yes, you have to do the work. You have to show up on the first date, sit at the computer to write, make time to exercise, eat healthy food, make the calls, and set up the interview for a new job, but you're not doing it alone. Your inspiration, your guidance, and your power come from Divine Source.

When you have consciously accepted your connection and you know that you are Divine Source energy having a human experience, how do you go about receiving what you want?

The first how-to-manifest, or receive, teachings that became popular in the West were found in the book *Think and Grow Rich* by Napolean Hill. The metaphysical concept of vibration was edited out of the book, because when the book was published in 1937, the public probably wasn't quite ready for it. According to Jerry Hicks, who found an original copy of the book and compared it to the one that was published and widely distributed, it said things like we are vibrational beings and that this is a vibrational Universe. I'm still not sure that today most people are ready to embrace this concept—even though it's true.

Then, we had the Seth teachings. These teachings are brilliant, but the books are huge and dense. I spent my midthirties engrossed in them. I loved them. Seth shared with us that our thoughts create our reality (vibration and energy spoken of again) and that we are more than just human; we are souls who make choices about our lifetimes.

In the eighties and nineties and continuing today, many have written and lectured on manifesting (or receiving). The following is my attempt to consolidate the brilliant teachings of many amazing teachers so that you can begin now to receive the gifts you desire. Here is what you need to know:

In order to receive, you have to be a vibrational match with what you've asked for (the same way you have to turn the channel to your local PBS channel if you want to watch PBS), meaning your energy and thoughts need to be aligned to that which you desire. What this basically means is that you can't receive love if you think you're unworthy of love. You can't receive money or ideas or anything else if you don't understand you are worthy, because you are Divine Source energy in human form. You have to feel good about receiving what you've asked for. If this isn't yet clear to you, don't worry. I will explain all of this in more depth.

FIVE STEPS TO RECEIVING

1 **Know that you come from Divine Source energy.** This means that even though you're in your body, you are still mostly Divine Source energy in human form. And because of that, you are innately lovable, worthy, creative, loved, valued, cared about, looked after, and given to by Divine Source. You draw to you that which you want because of how powerful you really are as an extension of Divine Source energy in physical form. Any thoughts to the contrary of your worth and lovability come from the small part of you that is human (your ego, which can stand for *Edging God Out*) and filters thoughts, conversations, and events through your human mind —the ego—rather than through your Divine Source energy being.

2 **Ask for what you want.** To do this, you have to be clear and specific about what you want and why you want it. You have to focus on the positive! Focus on the feeling of what it feels like to have what you want. Here's a huge key: Don't expect that having things or certain people in your life will make you feel better about yourself. You have to feel better about yourself first, and then choose to have those things. Things or people will never make you feel better about yourself. You do that job. And once you feel better about yourself, you can receive whatever you desire.

3 **Understand that your thoughts create your reality.** As Abraham shares with us through Esther Hicks, "You get what you think about whether you want it or not."

So a thought of "I'm lovable, worthy, valued, cared for"

allows you to attract more love and money into your life. A thought of "I'm not lovable or worthy, but I want the Universe to send me a man to validate me," will keep you from receiving the gift of a precious man to share love with and keep you from receiving money.

Remember you get what you think about, whether it's what you want or not. Your thoughts carry a vibration—energy—and the Universe responds to that vibration, that energy. This is a vibrational Universe. Everything responds to energy or vibration.

So given that every single one of us has negative or contradictory thoughts that slow or block the flow, how do we stop and change those thoughts? First, you have to be willing to change the payoff of negative thinking. Payoffs can be safety, protection, the easy way out, manipulation, and so on.

Let's assume you're willing to allow Divine Source to protect you and keep you safe; you no longer have a need to block love or money from coming to you as a means of safety and protection from having your heart broken or your money lost or misspent.

Second, you have to be willing to think positive thoughts. You can't play victim here and win. Life doesn't work that way. So be willing to be a hero in your own life story. Be willing to be victorious in your learning, not a victim of your circumstances.

4 **Receive with appreciation.** Graciously accept the gifts that come to you. Accept your friend's offer to pay for lunch. Accepting things from others is where many people get tripped up: If you don't understand that you are Divine

Source energy in human form, you might not feel worthy to receive. Abraham shares with us that if you have any sense of unworthiness, you will muddy the water and slow down, if not stop, the flow of things to you.

Here's the final step of the secret to receiving:

5 **Be in a place in your mind and heart where you feel good.** To receive what you've asked for and what you haven't even thought of asking for, you have to feel good about yourself and your life—no matter what your current reality is. You have to feel as if it's already here!

The recent Abraham teachings translated by Esther Hicks call this feeling-good place the vortex. The vortex is the place where you are aligned with who you really are—that is, Divine Source energy having a human/physical experience. What works for me is calling it My Feeling Good Place. Call it what you feel comfortable with; it's the same no matter what name we give it.

From this place, focus on what you want and how it will feel when it's here. Suppose you want to take a vacation and you've had a hard time allowing yourself to take the time off from work. See yourself happy and relaxed, and enjoying new sights, sounds, smells, tastes, people, and so on. See yourself coming back feeling alive and reenergized. Likewise, if you want to attract love, see yourself sharing love; feel what it will feel like to love someone and to receive their love. Feel what it will feel like to share things, places, ideas, and creations with that person and others. Daydream to your heart's content. If you want to attract a new career, feel what it will be like to be in a new job, doing work that you find meaningful, having your heart and spirit light up with joy and love, and having people around you who you value and who value you.

In order to receive anything you want, you have to act as if it's already here—a new house, car, husband, job, doctor . . . and then ask for what you want and stay with the feeling of having it. Then you have to let go of how, why, where, and when, and let Divine Source handle those.

The following is an Abraham quote that explains this concept perfectly:

> When you talk about *what* you want and *why* you want it, there's usually less resistance within you than when you talk about *what* you want and *how* you're going to get it. When you pose questions you don't have answers for, like *how, where, when, who,* it sets up a contradictory vibration that slows everything down.
> —Abraham, Excerpt from 2005 workshop in San Antonio, TX

In other words, get out of the way and focus on the feelings of having what you've asked for. It is Divine Source's job to handle getting it to you.

Notice the above quote doesn't say *not* to take any action. You want to take action, but the key is to be in your feeling-good place when you do. Do the affirmations, make the phone calls, answer the e-mails, talk to your kids, stop in and see someone—just do it all from a place of feeling good. Because if you're not feeling good, that's the energy—the vibration—you'll give off, and that will keep what you want away instead of drawing it to you.

Have you ever gone on a job interview when you felt

lousy? How did it go? Probably not well. Or, if you've gone out with a group of people and were feeling unhappy, you might have noticed that most of the people shied away from you and paid attention to people who exuded happiness. That's because people are drawn to other people's feeling-good energy. Yes, people are that sensitive, including men!

Here is a recap of the steps that are necessary to receive that which you want or desire:

1. Realize you are Divine Source energy in human form, which means you are worthy and lovable and connected.

2. Ask for what you want—be clear and specific, and then act as if it's already here.

3. Understand that your thoughts create your reality.

4. Receive with appreciation.

5. Get into a place in your heart and mind where you feel good.

In the next chapter, I'll share with you a technique I use to get into my feeling-good place. Remember, you just have to want to feel good more than you want to be right or in control or a victim. Those are just the ego's thoughts. And I know you want to live from your Divine Source energy place where you are fabulous!

Will it take practice? Yes. And you can do it. I have people write to me all the time saying that they tried it for an hour or during a date, or over a weekend, and were thrilled with the results.

Remember, you cannot force your way into feeling fabulous, your feeling-good place. You flow, glide, daydream, melt, float, or meditate your way into your feeling fabulous place, where you are aligned with your higher, Divine Source energy, fabulous self. And from that place you ask and receive what you desire.

— 27 —

Getting Into Your Feeling-Good Place, Morning & Night

To receive what you want and desire, to make healthy and meaningful decisions, to have productive conversations, to be guided to the right destination or person, to talk to an ailing friend, or to have an amazing interview or audition, you need to be in your feeling-good place. This is because from that place of calmness, connectedness, centeredness, groundedness, and joyfulness, you will hear your inner guidance and what another person is really saying to you. Morcover, your heart will be wide open, you'll be in the flow or the zone, and the joy you feel will come across in your actions and speech.

So the most important thing you want to do every day and night is to get into your feeling-good place. Why at night? So you'll sleep better, which gives you more opportunity to wake up feeling good. Then, before you get out of bed or start your day, get yourself into that place.

Here's what I do to feel good. I imagine myself floating in

God's arms. I see my "floating in God's arms" place as a clear, warm body of crystal-clear aquamarine water. Floating there, I'm warm and safe, and the sun is shining down on me. Dolphins and turtles swim near, and I am completely content and happy; I am filled with love and joy. God is in the water with her arms gently underneath me, or God is the water and the dolphins and the turtles. Angels join me too.

I keep a framed photograph of the ocean nearby to remind me that is where I feel happy, peaceful, and fabulous. When I look at that picture, I know instantly what that feels like, so I can imagine being there no matter what is going on in my life.

Come up with what works for you to create a feeling-good place. Maybe it's on a soaring red-rock mountaintop, or in a flower-filled field by a gently flowing stream, or in a dense forest under a giant redwood tree. It can be whatever place resonates with you. And then have a reminder—like my ocean picture—that allows you to get there quickly when you need to. Maybe for you it's a certain smell or texture—soft roses or silk. Or maybe it's a crystal you hold in your hand or next to your heart. Maybe it's a picture of a child or old man or woman with their soul's deep wisdom shining through their eyes. It can be anything that is a reminder of the feeling you have when you're safe, content, peaceful, happy, and fabulous.

Spend five to fifteen minutes every morning and evening just basking in this place. Be still and quiet or go for a peaceful, silent walk. The idea is to keep your mind calm and peaceful so you will feel fabulous.

Calmness, connectedness, centeredness, groundedness, and joyfulness—these qualities wait for you in your feeling-fabulous place, your feel-good place. Bask in this place morning and night and as often as possible during the day!

— 28 —

Setting Your Vibration to Receive

To set your vibration to easily and effortlessly receive what you want, try this daydream exercise, which is an entertaining activity that really works. In fact, it's one of the best ways to do this. First, get into your feeling-good place like we discussed in Chapter 27, and then let your mind daydream and imagine for fifteen minutes each day about new adventures, people, circumstances . . . anything you want to create in your life. The key here is to *feel* it in your daydream like it is really happening.

Let's say you are looking for your ideal partner or you want a new home with more room or a more rewarding job. Begin by daydreaming about all the details of your circumstances.

Let's start with a partner, or a new-and-improved version of the one you recently broke up with. See yourself with your new partner enjoying fun things together. Imagine in detail all the adventures you'll be sharing. Daydream about how it will feel to be doing these fun things. Then, focus on other things you'd like to do with this person. It could be any-thing—for instance, going to family events, to the movies, out to dinner, double dating, having long discussions about a powerful book, or sitting on a beach sipping a cocktail at sun-set. It could be anything that makes you feel good and puts you in the dream of the relationship you are creating. Let other relationships that you see or read or hear about add to the richness of your daydream.

If you want a new home, daydream about living there, having friends over, your family coming to visit, meditating in your special place, or sleeping in your bedroom. What does it look like? How do you feel when you are there? Day-dream about all the details.

Do the same with a new job. Imagine that you are doing work that is meaningful and joyful for you and that you are working in your perfect environment. What is that? What does it look like? How do you feel when you are there? Imag-ine a caring supervisor and supportive coworkers. Daydream about all the details. This job is out there, and you are creating being a vibrational match to it.

Have fun with this exercise and enjoy the results. It won't take you long to receive what you want if you do this faith-fully every day with positive intentions.

Make the time every day to joyously daydream for the sake of living your dream life! Allow yourself to easily and effortlessly receive all the gifts and joys life has to offer.

29

Lifestyle Necessities for Feeling Fabulous

To feel fabulous now and forever, there are many things you need to do in addition to all the suggestions you've received throughout this book. These things include physical exercise, a smart diet, and attention to your inner self through meditation and relaxation. And although this has been mentioned a few times in this book, it's essential to read from a spiritually uplifting book every day. This is a suggestion I cannot repeat too often!

Daily Reading

Many years ago, one of the teachers I met on my journey suggested that I read from a powerful spiritual book every morning. Implementing this advice was one of the most important steps I ever took, and now I *always* recommend it to my clients. (See page 159 for some of my favorite titles that can help you on your journey. These particular books have changed my life as well as the lives of many of my clients, friends, and family.) Every morning, perhaps when you are having coffee or tea, read three to five pages of your chosen book. Use a highlighter or add a page flag to highlight important phrases or sentences, and simply enjoy this method of learning. Doing this in the morning puts uplifting and meaningful information into your mind as you start your day. When you do this every day, by the end of a year you'll be amazed at how much you've learned. If you prefer, you can try audio books or inspirational DVDs. Choose the learning method that is most effective for you.

Physical Exercise

If you have the permission of your healthcare practitioner, choose one or more of the exercises below. If you cannot perform any of these exercises, ask your doctor to refer you to a physical therapist who can design a program that is suitable for you. Hiring a certified fitness trainer may also be a good idea for you. Be sure to get references.

Cardio is a must at least four times a week. I have never known a woman who feels fabulous who doesn't move her body a minimum of four times a week. Strength training is crucial for strong bones and effortlessly performing everyday functions. Core work is essential for your balance. The following are some great exercises for making you feel fabulous when you do them consistently:

- Swimming
- Walking
- Weight training
- Pilates
- Running
- Inline Skating
- Biking
- Dancing (Get some Zumba CDs and have fun!)
- Exercise classes with Hula-Hoops, balance balls, or BOSUs
- Dance classes

Stretch Daily

The only way to live comfortably in your body is to keep it loose. Get an exercise mat and put on your favorite television show while you stretch. Or better yet, put on some nice music while you ease into your stretches. If you've never taken a yoga class, now is a good time to join a beginner's class that focuses on relaxation and stretching. You can also purchase a DVD that leads you through beneficial stretches or you can buy a wonderful yoga DVD.

Smart Eating

Eating breakfast every day is crucial. I personally don't eat a big breakfast, but I do eat something every morning, even if it's only a quick protein drink. It is key to break your fast after sleeping. You'll want some carbohydrates to get your blood sugar up and some protein and a little fat to keep it steady throughout the morning until you eat lunch.

If you don't eat breakfast, or if you eat something with a lot of sugar, your blood sugar will usually crash around mid-morning. That's when you'll reach for something convenient to bring it back up. Convenient foods are usually sugary and full of carbohydrates. You'll wind up in a vicious cycle of high and low blood sugar, which always feels awful. Then lunch might not be so healthy. So, be sure to eat breakfast. And, of course, be sure to make healthy choices for all of your meals.

It's also a good idea to eat small portions of healthy food. Be aware of how much you are eating. When you go out to dinner, set aside half of your meal for the following day. Restaurant portions are usually much more than we need. When eating at home, make sure you are focusing on enjoying your meal. Don't multitask while you're eating, because if you do, you won't always know when you've eaten enough to satisfy your hunger. Eat slowly so that your stomach has time to let your brain know that it's full.

And finally, when it comes to drinking alcohol, less is more! The new research says that a glass of wine every day is good for you, but I choose not to drink during the week because I want my mind to be crystal clear when I'm coaching. But everyone is different. I truly enjoy cocktail hour with my husband on Friday night after work as well as a glass or two of wine on Saturday nights with dinner. You know what feels right for your body; just don't overdo it.

Meditation/Mind Relaxation

Give your mind the opportunity to relax every day. Just be still and quiet for fifteen minutes every day. Don't expect your mind to be quiet without practice. It won't be. Minds don't work that way, unless you spend an hour meditating every day training it to be quiet. A relaxed mind is a quieter mind, which is crucial to stress relief. We all need it. I'm sure you do something instinctively every day to try to quiet your mind without realizing it. I am now encouraging you to make it a daily and conscious choice. A wonderful meditation CD can be very helpful. So can just sitting and looking out at the trees or the ocean, depending on where you live. Just choose to be still and let yourself become peaceful.

Daily reading, stretching, meditation/relaxation, as well as regular exercise and eating small portions, are all necessary to feeling good. Make the health of your body, mind, and spirit your daily top priority, and soar with the joy of feeling fabulous.

— ৬ 30 ৫ —
What's Next?

Life coaching is a powerful and highly effective way to guide people to learn their true value, worth, gifts, and skills while at the same time helping them take appropriate action in their lives to fulfill their dreams. I became a certified life coach to help people who were stuck in loveless relationships or soul-draining jobs. All successful athletes have a coach to help them use their skills and strengths to the best of their ability and to win at their sport.

We can all use a coach to keep us positive and moving forward when things get tough or if we get stuck. I've found that coaching is the most powerful tool available to help you make the most of your life and your gifts.

On my website (www.carolchanel.com), you will find an offer to receive my free booklet, *The Seven Keys to Happiness and Fulfillment,* and to subscribe to my Rockin' Relationships e-zine. I know you will benefit from the information I share in *The Seven Keys.* In addition to other important keys to happiness, I discuss forgiveness, love, and trusting in a higher power in more depth.

As a complement to my motivational writing, I am a certified life coach who works one-on-one with my clients on a weekly basis to help them create exciting, joyful, loving, and lasting relationships. I also help them to create work that is meaningful and rewarding to them. While you are visiting my website, you can fill out a request to talk to me about the benefits of one-on-one coaching. While I don't coach everyone who contacts me, I will refer you to someone or to a type of work that could be beneficial for you.

Visit www.carolchanel.com.

Conclusion

It is my sincerest wish that the information in this book has helped you shift into a new and fabulous perspective of yourself. I also hope it has taught you how to feel that way forever.

Sometimes things will occur in your life that might make you forget you're fabulous. If you forget, don't worry; it's not permanent. Be compassionate with yourself. Part of feeling fabulous is being compassionate with yourself when life is difficult and you are sad or hurt. Fortunately for most of us, it's usually temporary. It's not easy to feel fabulous when you're in the middle of something that is challenging to deal with or that unsettles you. So give yourself a chance to handle what needs to be handled. To help you along your way, do something nice for yourself like taking a long bath or getting a massage. Cry if you feel the need to cry, talk to a caring friend, and allow yourself to heal. Then, read a relevant chapter in this book and get yourself back on track.

Remember that feeling fabulous isn't a fake feeling or feeling like you're on top of the world when you're not. It's feeling genuinely good about the whole of you—your emotions, your body, your heart, and your spirit.

The way I look at it (and how I teach my clients to look at it), you have a choice. You can feel fabulous or you can choose to not feel fabulous. Choose fabulous! It will serve you every day to make that choice.

Visit my website www.carolchanel.com and download my free booklet *The Seven Keys to Happiness and Fulfillment.* I encourage you to also sign up for my free e-zines about relationships with yourself and others to keep getting inspired to new levels of feeling fabulous and having great relationships from that feeling-good place.

Joyfully,
Carol

A Note from the Author

I feel fabulous almost all the time now, but I didn't always feel that way. I know that my own journey to this joyful and peaceful place was guided and aided by amazing women and men who taught me how to get and stay here. I'm sure I came in full of joy and light, just as all precious humans do. I can look at pictures of myself as a baby and little girl and see the joy. However, I had a challenging and painful childhood. I was hit by a car when I was five and almost died from major injuries. My mother died when I was seven, and when I was nine, my father married a woman who didn't like me. My father was a strict disciplinarian—a military officer—and didn't know how to nurture and guide a child or love one as different as I was. And my older brother did some unfortunate things to me when I was very young. I didn't have anyone I could turn to who would help me. I asked neighbors, friends, and family, but no one would help.

I know that it is because of my painful childhood that I became fascinated in psychology. I earned a degree in sociology with an area of specialization in criminology and a minor in psychology. My plan was to rehabilitate juvenile delinquents, but the system wasn't really set up to do that. So by the time I was in my twenties, I didn't like myself. In addition, I was convinced that I was ugly.

Fortunately, my powerful inner voice wouldn't be silenced, and I was always seeking to grow and love. In 1975 I took a solo trip around the world and explored some amazing cultures and places. In the process, I learned so much about others and myself that I was able to shed a huge layer of pain from my heart and soul.

But even after that experience, deep down I still thought I was ugly, and I wasn't happy. I basically tried to commit suicide by starving myself and almost died at age twenty-eight from the complications of anorexia. I had exercised and starved myself almost beyond repair. But once again, something clicked, and I sought help. My brother actually came to my aid, and I stayed with him while I got medical help and repaired my body.

In my late thirties, after a lot of therapy, I turned all of my early trauma into some huge positives in my life. For one thing, I have a depth of compassion that seems to only come from going through tough times. I met a brilliant spiritual teacher who was a behavioral psychologist; he told me that everything I had experienced was "for the purpose of knowing at a cellular level what other people were feeling so I could truly help them." He was right, and from that moment on, I never felt like a victim again. We are either victims of our circumstances or victorious in our learning. God bless him—and thank you, God, for sending him to me. I would not be where I am without his insight.

The Universe has sent me many amazing, powerful souls to teach me and guide me on my path to joy and feeling fabulous. I've been given the gift of Grace and was able to heal my relationship with my stepmother before she passed, understand my father, forgive my brother, forgive myself, and see how God and my angels have always been there watching out for me.

I have been on this path of spiritual study for more than thirty years now. I've learned powerful concepts and have received the gifts of understanding, wisdom, vision, and a powerful intuition over the years.

Once I healed, I met and married a beautiful man and spirit, my dear Robert. His support and belief in me have kept me going through life's inevitable rough times and normal challenges. He always sees the glass half full, and when you're on a path that is undefined and made up as you go, having a partner like that is a gift we all can ask for and all need.

I want you all to have your own Robert—a partner who believes in you, sees your light and beauty, and stands by you when you turn away from yourself until you find your way back to self-love.

So here I am, sixty-two years old, and I feel beautiful, sexy, joyful, and full of life. I'm thrilled I never succumbed to my pain and desire to leave this body. It's a good body, and it's been through a lot. I never criticize it now. How can I criticize magnificence? It's the vessel I get to be in for the remainder of this lifetime, and I'm very happy to have it because I know one day I'll be back in spirit form.

So love your body (or at least be kind to it) and acknowledge its brilliance—as well as the brilliance of its creator and your choice to be here now. It's a perfect choice!

**Enjoy this life! It's meant to be lived,
and you are meant to feel fabulous!
So feel fabulous forever!**

Recommended Reading

This is a list of my favorite spiritual books. I put them in the order I usually recommend my clients read them. These books have changed my life and the lives of my clients. I hope you enjoy them!

The Power of Intention by Dr. Wayne Dyer (Hay House Inc. 2004)

The Four Agreements by don Miguel Ruiz (Amber-Allen Publishing 1997)

The Vortex by Esther and Jerry Hicks (Hay House Inc. 2009)

Taming Your Gremlin by Richard Carson (Harper Perennial 1983, 2003)

Excuses Begone by Dr. Wayne Dyer (Hay House Inc. 2009)

Radical Forgiveness, Second Edition by Colin Tipping (Global 13 Publications 2002)

The Power of Now by Eckhart Tolle (New World Library 1999)

Seat of the Soul by Gary Zukav (Simon & Schuster 1990)

Care of the Soul by Thomas Moore (HarperPerennial 1992)

Journey of the Heart by John Welwood (HarperPerennial 1991)

A Return to Love by Marianne Williamson (HarperCollins 1992)

A Woman's Worth by Marianne Williamson (Random House 1993)

The Path to Love by Deepak Chopra (Harmony Books 1997)

Loving What Is by Byron Katie (Harmony Books 2002)

Nutrition

Eat Right for Your Type by Peter D'Adamo (G.P. Putnam's Sons 1996)

Meditation

Getting Into the Vortex by Esther and Jerry Hicks (Hay House Inc. 2010)

Meditation for Beginners by Jack Kornfield (Sounds True 2004)

Exercise

Stretching, 30th Anniversary Edition by Bob Anderson (Shelter Publications 2010)

Rodney Yee's Yoga for Beginners DVD by Rodney Yee (Gaiam 2009)

Absolute Abs by JJ Flizanes (Morris Book Publishing 2011)

Style

The Triumph of Individual Style: A Guide to Dressing Your Body, Your Beauty, Your Self by Carla Mason Mathis (Fairchild 2002)

Acknowledgments

I would like to acknowledge Carol Killman Rosenberg, my editor and positive force behind this project. Carol took my ideas and my short, punchy, and often incomplete sentence writing style and turned the manuscript into a cohesive and flowing whole. This book would not have been possible without her experience, wise voice, and positive energy. Thank you from the bottom of my heart!

I would like to acknowledge Gary Rosenberg who caringly and patiently created my covers and laid out this book. You wouldn't be reading this without his vision, experience, and gifts.

I would also like to acknowledge the amazingly talented and awesome Janet Davis for her fabulous cover art.

To my precious husband, Robert, who never stops encouraging me and believing in me. From day one, you have been my source of inspiration and joy. I love you, and I'm eternally appreciative of you. God bless you!

To all my clients over the years who trusted me and trusted yourselves to remember that you are fabulous women. I am so blessed to have had your energy, kindness, openness, light, and love. Thank you!

About the Author

Carol Chanel is a certified personal and professional life coach. She has a B.A. in sociology with an area of specialization in criminology and a minor in psychology. She has worked in the self-improvement field for more than thirty years. She has written extensively on the subject of self-esteem, relationships, love, empowerment, and spirituality and maintains an extensive archive of materials on her website, www.carolchanel.com.